WORKING TOGETHER IN THE 1990s

A Guide For Local Authorities And Housing Associations

Ross Fraser

Foreword

Central Government has determined that future provision of social housing should rest with the housing association movement. A watershed will be reached in 1991/92 when for the first time housing association completions should be twice that of local authorities. This does not mean that local authorities can opt out of their statutory requirements to house the homeless and plan strategically for future housing provision in their areas.

The objective of this book is to assist both housing associations and local authorities to work together effectively. This is a very practical document which describes ways in which local authorities and housing associations can co-operate and, for each of the topic areas, gives actual examples of successful schemes.

It is thus a useful, if not exhaustive, checklist for both practitioners and members of management committees in both sectors who are looking for ways of developing social housing or improving liaison. If you wish to pursue one or more of the schemes that are in the book please contact the originating organisation rather than the Institute of Housing.

Dennis Sullivan
Chairman of the IOH Steering Group Supervising this publication

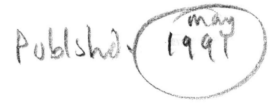

Publshd may 1991

Contents

Acknowledgements

The author would like to thank the following people for their valuable assistance.

Project Steering Group

Dennis Sullivan (Royal Borough of Kensington And Chelsea), Sue Ellenby (Family Housing Association), Ken Bartlett (Housing Corporation), Mark Lupton (IOH), David Seviour (Leicester Housing Association), Paul Smith (Cardiff City Council) and Mel Usher (then Blackburn MBC)

Sale of Local Authority Land

Robin Lawler (Leeds Partnership Homes), Bernadette Marjoram (LB Lambeth) and various members of the steering group.

Use of Planning Powers

Kathleen Dunmore and Valli van Zijl (Social Housing Unit of the House Builders Federation), Andy Moore (Rural Housing Trust), Ian Stuart (New Islington and Hackney Housing Association), Lesley Dixon (Cumbria Rural Housing Group), Frank Vickery (East London Housing Association), Christopher Guy (Basingstoke District Council), Peter Davey (Circle 33 Housing Trust), Richard Bate (National Housing And Town Planning Council) and George Nicholson (CHICL).

Financial Assistance to Housing Associations

Siobhan McDonough (London Borough of Merton councillor), Keith Exford (Wandle Housing Association), Kathy Bucknall (LB Merton), Michael Hill (Countryside Developments PLC), Martin Field (Leicester City Council)

Stock Transfer

Geoff Brooks (Ryedale Housing Association), Rob Orme (Knowlsey MBC), Sue Bickler (TPAS), Mark Klienman and John Hills (London School of Economics), Terry Mitchell (Newbury DC), Bob Williams (housing consultant)

Special Needs Housing

Peter Mountford Smith (SITRA), Stephen Cook (St Edmundsbury DC), Jerry Hughes (East London Housing Association), Jenny Brierley (South Yorkshire Housing Association), Martin Cox (Look Ahead Housing Association), Brian Mathews (Wandle Housing Association), Paul Ballat (London Borough of Wandsworth), Julie Harrison (Ealing Family Housing Association), Jane Everton and Jane Luby (Housing Corporation), Mark Beard, Liz Taylor and Cliff Prior (all Stonham Housing Association).

Urban Renewal

Ann Petherick (Living Over The Shop project), Gillian Ross (Foundation Housing Association), John Perry (Institute Of Housing), Ann Branson, Ita Cooke, and Chris Ingham (all Leicester City Council), Steve Gough (London Borough of Lambeth)

Local Authority Services

Albert Rowley (East London Housing Association), Dennis Sullivan and Michael Baldwin (Royal Borough of Kensington and Chelsea)

Joint Training Initiatives

Margaret Smith (IOH), Margaret Sandford (IOH), Kim Everitt (Imperial College), Halina Goodall (NEHAGTS), Lesley Dixon (Cumbria Rural Housing Group), Rosalind Dean (housing consultant)

Nomination Agreements

Jeanette Yorke (London Housing Unit), Brian Rooney (London Borough Of Lewisham), Oona Hickson (then NFHA)

Housing Benefit

Bill Irvine (Strathclyde Regional Council), Dave Addy (Leicester City Council), Jane McGarry (IOH) and Sue Ellenby (Family Housing Association)

Thanks to Nigel Armstrong (Housing Corporation), Bob Ryder, Jon Rouse, Lesley Creedon, Peter Clark, Liz Walton, Joanne Gibson, Marie Winckler, Brian Webber, Alistair Bishop, Hugh Corner, Nick Simon and Seamus Gillen (all DoE) for their comments and assistance.

Thanks to Ashley Costello, Pat Simpson and John Perry (all IOH) for producing the publication and to Janey Sugden (Artworkers) for designing it.

Thanks to Dave Treanor (NFHA), Michael Ashley (ADC), Marianne Hood (TPAS), Nick Raynsford (housing consultant) and Steve Wilcox (housing consultant) for their general help and encouragement.

Special thanks to Mark Lupton (IOH) for commissioning the publication, Lorainne Dore (IOH) for her excellent administrative support and Les Fraser for acting as a 'lay reader' of the text.

All errors and opinions are the responsibility of the author.
Ross Fraser
May 1991

INTRODUCTION

In 1985, the Institute of Housing published a report entitled 'Local Authorities And Housing Associations: Working Together'. Much of the text is still relevant today and we do not seek to duplicate it here.
Instead, this publication seeks to:

■ provide an update on developments which have occurred in the last six years

■ suggest new areas of partnership that may become important in the next decade

■ highlight examples of what is already being achieved by local authorities and housing associations working together.

Such are the range of partnership possibilities that this publication cannot, and will not try to, include them all. Instead, it will concentrate on what the Institute of Housing believes are the most fruitful areas for local authorities and housing associations to work together.

The publication is intended for use by local authority councillors and staff (in housing, planning, social services, environmental health, finance and all other departments which have contact with housing associations) and housing association committee members and staff, in England.

In most cases the technical information we have present applies to Wales as well as England. Where this is not the case, we say so. However, the policy framework in which the Welsh Office and Tai Cymru apply these regulations is sometimes significantly different. Welsh readers should, therefore, contact the Welsh Office and Tai Cymru to check on policy matters before proceeding with specific schemes.

We also hope that local authority and housing association tenants and anyone with an interest in social housing will find the publication useful.

The publication is intended to be as easy-to-read as possible. However, as much of the text involves the interpretation of complex and sometimes arcane government regulations, there are inevitably passages which are more difficult to read than others. We have tried to illuminate the technical material by providing examples of actual initiatives. Where possible, we have also introduced simple flow diagrams.

By intention, the publication is practical rather than theoretical. This is not because the Institute wishes to avoid key issues such as the affordability of rents, the future of the housing association movement and the role of local authorities as housing providers or enablers. These issues have already been discussed in some detail in the Institute publication 'Social Housing In The 1990's', which was published in May 1990. Some of the issues will be subject to fresh scrutiny in a publication on the local authority 'enabling' role which is due to be published by the Institute, in conjunction with Longmans, in 1992.

This publication has a different purpose. It been produced in response to a constant demand from Institute members, employed by local authorities and housing associations, for practical guidance on the opportunities for authorities and associations to work together.

To appreciate the context in which 'working together' will take place, it is necessary to turn briefly to the major legislative and financial changes that have occurred since that 1985 report.

Social Housing: Changes In the Financial Arrangements

Since 1988 the main providers of social housing - local authorities and housing associations - have experienced radical changes in the financial regimes under which they operate.

For housing associations, the Housing Act 1988 has been the critical piece of legislation. The Act introduced fixed levels of Housing Association Grant (HAG), transferred a significant amount of financial risk to associations and created a new form of assured tenancy for all new housing association tenants.

For local authorities, the Local Government and Housing Act 1989 has also had a major impact. Regarding revenue expenditure, the Act has prevented the transfer of funds between the Housing Revenue Account and the General Fund, amalgamated housing and rent rebate subsidy, linked rents to capital values and revised the overall calculation of subsidy entitlement. Regarding capital expenditure, the Act has tightened controls over local authority borrowing, further restricted their ability to re-invest capital receipts for housing provision and linked borrowing approvals to levels of capital receipts.

The cumulative impact of this legislation has been as follows.

Many housing associations have switched from the rehabilitation of existing property to the less risky business of new build. The Department of the Environment is about to commission a major research project to investigate the full extent of this trend. In addition, small and specialist associations are increasingly relying on larger asset-rich associations to raise finance and undertake development on their behalf. A number of associations are considering merger with other associations in order to become more effective developers of housing. Finally, according to research conducted by the National Federation of Housing Associations, rents on new assured lettings rose by almost 20% during 1990-1 (the first full year that the mixed funding regime has been in effect).

The traditional role of local authorities as providers of low cost rented housing has been placed under severe strain. Authorities which, due to substantial Right To Buy receipts, had escaped the full impact of earlier borrowing restrictions now find that their ability to build new homes is almost non-existent. Authorities with low levels of receipts have faced this problem since the early 1980's. By merging different forms of housing subsidy, the government has gained control over local authority rent levels and is forcing them upwards. Many authorities are now levying a 'secondary' rent increase as a revenue contribution to the cost of modernising existing homes. Most authorities fear that the recalculation of subsidy entitlement will reduce the finance available for management and maintenance and thus place them in the invidious position of charging higher rents for a declining housing service.

These restrictions upon local authority housing expenditure are not accidental. They are the means by which the government intends to transform authorities from 'providers' of new subsidised rented housing (often known generically as social housing) into 'enablers' who help other landlords to meet this need. The government has encouraged housing associations, which it defines as part of the 'independent rented sector', to take on the role of primary providers of new subsidised rented housing. However, even with the increase in the availability of Housing Corporation capital funding and the introduction of private finance, new housing association building is unlikely to approach the number of homes needed by homeless and badly housed people. Readers are again referred to 'Social Housing In The 1990's' for a more detailed discussion of these issues.

The irony of the government's policy is that responsibility for securing accommodation for homeless people will continue to rest with local authorities. Although local authorities will continue to be the major social landlord in most areas, responsibility for the homeless can only be adequately discharged with increased support and assistance from housing associations. Effective arrangements for local authority nomination of homeless households to housing association property have become essential. Conversely, housing associations will have to rely on assistance from authorities (in the form of land, use of planning powers and financial assistance) if they are to develop housing which homeless people and others in housing need can afford.

The Local Authority 'Enabling Role'

This developing relationship between authorities and associations - mirrored by similar arrangements with private landlords and developers - gives expression to the government's concept of local authorities as 'enablers'.

This 'enabling' role has been the subject of much debate. Many commentators have pointed out that increased restrictions upon the use of capital receipts, coupled with new 'debt redemption' rules, make it more difficult for local authorities to assist housing associations. Moreover, any financial assistance authorities give to housing associations will directly compete with the spending required to repair and improve their own housing stock.

By appointing the Audit Commission to determine whether the current financial and legislative environment provides a suitable framework for 'enabling' local authorities, the government tacitly accepts that it may not. The Audit Commission's recommendations are eagerly awaited. However, their study will not be completed until late 1991 and resulting legislation or regulations are unlikely to be in place until 1993 at the earliest.

Until then, local authority assistance will be confined to the use of existing powers and closer working relationships with housing associations. Indeed, as this publication demonstrates, many local authorities have been acting as 'enablers' long before the government latched onto the concept.

Scope For Working Together

The underlying themes of this publication are as follows.

Notwithstanding varying perceptions of the 'role' of local authorities and housing associations, it is essential for these parties to work together if affordable housing for rent or shared ownership is to be provided for people who cannot afford to buy their own homes.

There are areas where improved liaison between authorities and associations can substantially improve the provision of housing services to existing tenants.

The ability of local authorities to provide this help will be enhanced if they develop a corporate strategy for 'working together' which recognises the particular contribution that planning, social services, direct works and finance and housing department staff can make and ensures that these functions are effectively administered.

There is particular scope for local authorities to assist housing associations through:

■ the sale of local authority land at less than market value

■ the use of planning powers to help associations buy private sector land more cheaply

■ financial assistance towards the capital and revenue costs of projects

■ the transfer of local authority housing stock to associations

■ the use of urban renewal powers to assist associations working in town or city centre areas

■ co-ordination and assistance with the provision of special needs housing

■ provision of professional services to associations

There are clear benefits to be obtained from better liaison between authorities and associations over:

■ staff training

■ housing benefit payments

■ nomination agreements

The benefits of formalising arrangements for 'working together' will be examined in the concluding chapter.

NB. The term 'housing association' should, at all times, be assumed to refer solely to housing associations which are formally registered with the Housing Corporation.

1

SALES OF LOCAL AUTHORITY LAND TO HOUSING ASSOCIATIONS

The purpose of the chapter is to explain:

■ how the sale of local authority land to housing associations can help to produce more low cost housing

■ what legislative powers local authorities can use to sell land they own

■ what government approvals local authorities must obtain before selling land

■ the restrictions upon the ability of local authorities to spend money obtained from the sale of land

■ how local authorities can sell land cheaply in return for the right to nominate people in housing need to the homes which are built upon the land

■ how local authorities can purchase private sector land in order to assemble sites and sell them to housing associations

This chapter deals only with the sale of land. The sale of property is dealt with in the chapter on 'Stock Transfer'.

Importance Of Local Authority Land Sales For Housing Associations

Local authorities have, in the past, acquired land for several reasons. In some cases the land has been purchased, under powers now contained in Part 2 of the Housing Act 1985, with the intention of constructing low cost rented housing upon it. Other sites have been acquired as a result of Compulsory Purchase Orders with the intention of rehabilitating or clearing the unfit buildings which stand upon the land. For the sake of simplicity, this land is often referred to as 'housing land'. In other cases, land has been acquired for purposes which have nothing to do with the provision of general needs housing accommodation. For example, land may have been acquired to build or replace local authority owned residential homes or to facilitate the redevelopment of a town or city centre. This land is often referred to as 'non housing land.'

However, with their ability to undertake major housing or other capital projects severely constrained, many local authorities have reviewed the benefit of holding large banks of land. A number have decided that it would be more prudent to sell some or all of their land to housing associations. The primary benefits of doing so are as follows.

Local authorities gain by being able to nominate people in housing need to the new homes built by associations on this land.

Housing associations gain because they obtain a more predictable supply of land for development. And, if the land is sold at less than market value, less of their HAG funding is needed to buy it. Associations can therefore use the 'surplus' HAG within their allocation to build more homes or buy more sites. This process is commonly known as 'HAG stretch'.

Under regulations introduced in 1990, local authorities can also purchase land with the express purchase of assembling sites for development and selling them to housing associations.

The sale of local authority land to housing associations is thus of mutual benefit. However, it is subject to a plethora of government controls and regulations. Most important of these are the need to obtain DoE approval to sell land, particularly where the authority proposes to sell at less than market value, and the DoE 'debt redemption' rules which severely constrain the ability of local authorities to spend the money obtained from land sales. It is to these complex issues that we now turn our attention.

Legislation covering the sale of Local Authority Land

This section outlines the legislative powers which local authorities can use to sell land and the approvals (known as 'consents') that they need to obtain from the government before doing so.

■ Non Housing Land

Section 123 of the Local Government Act 1972 gives local authorities a general power to dispose of land held for non housing purposes.

The term 'general power' means that if a local authority's proposals meet these criteria, specific DoE consent is not required before the authority can proceed. The term 'general consent' is also used in this context and has the same meaning.

However, if local authority land is sold at less than the 'best consideration reasonably obtainable', the specific consent of the DoE is required. The term 'best consideration' means open market value, taking into account any restrictive covenants or conditions of sale.

■ Housing Land

Section 32 of the Housing Act 1985 requires specific consent for the disposal of land held for housing purposes under Part 2 of that Act.

These consents will primarily be required for the sale of land at less than market value, as the DoE has given a general consent for the sale of land (on which no dwellings have been erected) at 'best consideration'.

Sale Of Land At Less Than Market Value

When considering whether to give consent to the sale of land at less than market value, the DoE will require information in order to assess the market value of the land. When providing this information, local authorities should present one set of figures which ignore the financial impact of nomination rights or planning agreements. A second set of figures should also be presented, containing information about the land value after these factors have been included. This will enable the DoE to assess the full impact of the discount - which is known as a 'gratuitous benefit'. The term 'gratuitous benefit' also applies to other forms of subsidy such as grants or loans.

Under Section 25 of the Local Government Act 1988, local authorities require the specific consent of the DoE where they are proposing to sell land at less than market value in order to facilitate the development of rented housing on that land. Most sales of land at less than market value to housing associations will be targeted towards the provision of rented housing.

However, the DoE has granted a 'general consent' for the provision of gratuitous benefits (such as the sale of land at less than market value) if shared ownership homes are to be built as a result. The general consent comes with the proviso that the purchaser of the property must buy at least a 99 year lease and a minimum stake of 25% of the equity (value) of the property.

When deciding whether to grant consent for the sale of land at less than market value, or indeed for any other form of gratuitous benefit, the DoE will also take into account the level of public subsidy which the resulting housing scheme will attract.

The DoE stipulates that any 'gratuitous benefit' provided by a local authority towards the provision of rented housing by a housing association must not take the total level of public subsidy any higher than the amount of HAG funding that the Housing Corporation would provide for similar housing schemes in that area of the country. This subsidy limit applies to any combination of HAG, local authority capital or revenue grant, the value of any discount on the value of the land sold or any other form of public subsidy.

For example, if a housing association rented dwelling has a unit cost of £100,000 and the local HAG rate for that type of dwelling is 75% of costs, the maximum subsidy allowed is £75,000. Thus the local authority cannot provide more than 75% subsidy for the scheme, through any combination of discounted land or financial assistance.

Again, shared ownership schemes are treated differently. There is no upper limit on the level of local authority subsidy towards shared ownership schemes.

Further rules apply where a housing association project is being financed through a combination of local authority subsidy and HAG (provided by either the Housing

Sale of Local Authority Land

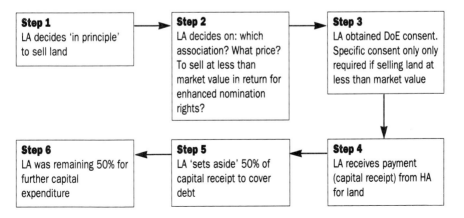

Step 1	Step 2	Step 3
LA decides 'in principle' to sell land	LA decides on: which association? What price? To sell at less than market value in return for enhanced nomination rights?	LA obtained DoE consent. Specific consent only only required if selling land at less than market value

Step 6	Step 5	Step 4
LA was remaining 50% for further capital expenditure	LA 'sets aside' 50% of capital receipt to cover debt	LA receives payment (capital receipt) from HA for land

Corporation or the local authority itself). Any HAG payable will be abated if, when combined with local authority subsidy, it would cause the total public subsidy to exceed the amount of HAG funding that the Housing Corporation would provide for similar housing schemes in that area of the country. This rule applies to both rented and shared ownership schemes.

Thus, if the local HAG rate for a dwelling which costs £100,000 to build is 75%, and the local authority discounts the land price by £10,000, the amount of HAG paid will be limited to £65,000 (65% of costs).

This means that the sale of local authority land at less than market value cannot be used to 'top up' any HAG to reduce rents.

However, as noted earlier, the subsidy will enable associations to 'stretch' the HAG and make it cover more units or schemes. From a Housing Corporation perspective, this will increase HAG 'value for money'. Any housing association bid for HAG made under these circumstances stands a better chance of obtaining Corporation approval.

Restrictions upon the ability of Local Authorities to spend money obtained from the sale of land

A key consideration for local authorities considering the sale of land is the amount of money from the proceeds of the sale - commonly known as the capital receipt - which can be re-invested in housing provision or other forms of activity.

In order to restrict the ability of local authorities to spend these capital receipts, further controls have been introduced by the government.

Under Section 59 of the Local Government and Housing Act 1989, English local authorities must 'set aside' 50% of any capital receipt from land sales for the purpose of debt redemption. This is known as the 'reserved' part of the capital receipt. Debt redemption involves all local authority debt - not just the element related to housing expenditure.

The term 'set aside' means that the debt need not be repaid but that the reserved part of the receipt must simply 'cover' the debt, that is, be available for repayment should the authority wish to do so. The reason that authorities may not wish to pay off existing debt is that the debt may have been obtained at low levels of interest and thus it may be more prudent to invest 'reserved' receipts at the higher rates of interest now current.

The remaining 50% of the receipt is known as the 'useable' part because it can be used for re-investment in housing or other forms of capital expenditure.

Thus, for example, if land with a market value of £200,000 is sold, the local authority will have to set aside £100,000 (50% of the receipt) for debt redemption. Only £100,000 will be useable for other capital expenditure.

In Wales, local authorities do not have to set aside any part of a capital receipt obtained from the sale of housing land. The sale of non housing land, however, requires 50% of the capital receipt to be set aside for debt redemption.

Under Regulation 14 and Schedule 1 of the Local Authority (Capital Finance) Regulations 1990, an authority which has no outstanding debt is not generally required to set aside any proportion of capital receipts for debt redemption. Local authorities without debt will generally be those which have paid off their debt through the transfer of their entire housing stock to a housing association. (See chapter on 'Stock Transfer' for further discussion).

It is now time to turn to the most complex rule regarding the sale of land.

Under Section 61 of the Local Government Act 1989, the aforementioned debt redemption rules are applied to the sale of land at less than market value. Section 61 states that 50% of the market value of the land must be set aside to cover debt even if the land is sold at less than market value. In effect, the discount is ignored when the 'reserved' and 'useable' parts of the receipt are being calculated.

The impact of Section 61 is best demonstrated by reference to the simple example given above.

If land with a market value of £200,000 is sold (at undervalue) for £180,000, the local authority will still have to reserve £100,000 for debt redemption. Its 'useable' receipt will thus only be £80,000.

When Section 61 was proposed, during the parliamentary passage of the Act, serious concern was expressed by local authorities and housing associations. They pointed out that Section 61 would penalise the authority by reducing its 'useable' receipt by the amount of any discount on the land price. Section 61 would thus act as a major disincentive towards the sale of local authority land at undervalue to housing associations. This, in turn, would reduce the opportunities to enhance the 'value for money' of HAG through the 'HAG stretch' mechanism.

Fortunately, as a result of concerted lobbying, the government backed down slightly - but only with respect to land sales to housing associations. All land sales to other bodies are still covered by Section 61 in its unamended form.

The government concession appeared in the Local Authority (Capital Finance) Regulations 1990. Regulation 20(4) exempts local authorities from having to reserve 50% of non-monetary consideration received in the form of nomination rights to the homes which are built on the land.

This complex concept is again best explained with reference to our simple example. If land with a market value of £200,000 is sold to a housing association (at undervalue) for £180,000, and the local authority obtains nomination rights worth £20,000, the local authority will only have to reserve £90,000 for debt redemption. Its 'useable' receipt will thus be £90,000.

In practice, almost every sale of local authority land at less than market value is now undertaken in return for nomination rights.

Valuation Of Nomination Rights

Two issues arise from the discounting of land in return for nomination rights.

The first concerns the level of nomination rights which the DoE is prepared to approve. For a detailed discussion of this issue see the chapter on 'Nomination Agreements'.

The other issue concerns the method of valuing nomination rights.

There is no clear DoE guidance on this matter and it will be up to local authorities to make their own valuation. Each local authority will, of course, have to satisfy the District Auditor that it has received sufficient consideration for the land and has not overvalued the nomination rights. The authority may also wish to take legal advice to satisfy itself that its proposals are not ultra vires.

The DoE, in contrast, does not require a formal valuation for the purposes of consent under Section 25 of the Local Government Act 1988. Local authorities are simply required to submit details of how nominations have been valued.

Land Assembly And Resale

In the introduction to this chapter, we noted that the recent DoE regulations have made it attractive for local authorities to buy land with the express intention of selling it on to housing associations. This type of activity gives practical expression to the local authority 'enabling role' referred to in the introductory chapter. The incentive is contained in Regulation 15 of the Local Authority (Capital Finance) Regulations 1990. Regulation 15 can also be combined with Regulation 20 which provides an incentive for local authorities to sell unused land which they already own to housing associations and in order to acquire other, more useful, land.

The Regulations do this by allowing the authority to deduct expenditure related to these activities from the capital receipt obtained from the property sale, leaving a smaller residual receipt from which 50% has to be set aside for debt redemption.

Under Regulation 15, where a local authority acquires land and disposes of it within 2 years of acquisition (or three years if a contract to dispose of it is entered into within two years of acquisition), the local authority can deduct the cost of the land from the receipt obtained from its disposal.

Thus if a local authority sells land which cost £400,000 to a housing association for £800,000, the cost of acquisition can be deducted from the sale receipt. The debt redemption calculation is then made on the basis that the sale receipt was only £400,000. Following the Section 59 principles explained earlier, 50% of the £400,000 must be set aside to cover debt and 50% is 'useable' for further capital expenditure.

Under Regulation 20, where unused land is disposed of in return for land on which there are no buildings, and the land received is of equal value, no reserved part needs to be set aside in respect of land received. However, any 'profit' is subject to reserved part rules. In this context, 'unused land' means land which for two years before the disposal had not been used for the purpose for which it had been held.

Thus if a local authority sells a site to a housing association for £200,000 and uses the receipt to buy another site for the same price, no money need be set aside for debt redemption. However, if the local authority sells a site for £200,000 and buys another site for £150,000, it must set aside £25,000 to cover debt and can use £25,000 on further capital expenditure.

There is a general consent to disposals of land acquired under Regulations 15 and 20. It is for each local authority to determine, with the assistance of their legal advisers and their auditor, whether or not particular transactions come within the terms of the regulations. Consents or approvals are not required from the DoE.

Example

A land for nominations deal
Cardiff City Council and Hafod Housing Association

Background
In 1973, Cardiff City Council earmarked a substantial site at the east of the city for the development of new housing and community facilities. The City Council hoped that 5,000 dwellings could be built on the site, providing accommodation for up to 18,000 people. By 1989 almost 3,000 dwellings had been constructed on the basis of a mix of homes for rent, shared ownership and outright ownership. A further 170 acres remained available for development.

Objectives
In January 1989 the City Council put 26 acres of land on the market - for sale by open competition to associations who would be prepared to develop social housing on it. A planning brief was provided setting out general parameters regarding density and open space and inviting tenders which specified proposals for the type of housing to be constructed, likely rent levels, nomination arrangements, subsidy requirements and so on.

Scheme Details
Following this competition, the City Council accepted a scheme proposed by Hafod Housing Association in association with Lovell Homes. Key elements of the successful scheme were as follows;

- 369 homes would be built for rent - mainly 2 or 3 bedroom houses but with a small number of 4 bedroom houses and some units for disabled people

- Hafod Housing Association was the only association to offer the City Council 100% nominations to initial lettings and relets

- In return, the land was to be provided at nil cost

- Initial rent levels were to average £43 per week with agreed increases of 6.5% per annum for 25 years

- Ownership of the rented homes would be vested in a fully mutual society set up by the Hafod Housing Association. Under the terms of Section 488 of the Income and Corporation Taxes Act 1988, the society was granted Welsh Office approval to obtain tax relief on the interest element of mortgage repayments on loans of up to £30,000 per unit of accommodation. This enabled the fully mutual society to charge lower rents than would otherwise have been possible.

- There was no financial support from Tai Cymru. Instead, construction costs were to be met through a combination of local authority grant funding, private sector cross subsidy and private borrowing by Hafod HA.

The Welsh Office approved the disposal as a 'homelessness initiative' and was therefore prepared to agree to 100% nomination rights for the local authority and to a corresponding reduction in the value of the land.

Example

A project involving Cross Subsidy from the sale of housing on the open market
Sale of land by Leicester City Council to Leicester Social Housing Consortium

The sale of local authority land to housing associations can produce social housing benefits in addition to those produced in 'discounted land for nominations' deals. Indeed, the following example does not involve any reduction in the price of local authority land at all.

Objectives
By selling a substantial amount of its landholding, on a phased basis, to a consortium of local housing associations, Leicester City Council was able to achieve the following objectives:

■ a large amount of Housing Corporation funding was committed to the city of Leicester

■ an inner-city site was sensitively redeveloped to meet the needs of black and ethnic minority people who live in that area

■ a large number of rented homes were provided at affordable rents on two sites in the city

The guarantee of a continued supply of reasonably priced land enabled the local housing associations which formed the Consortium to:

■ secure a large funding commitment from the Housing Corporation

■ use cross-subsidy of profits from the sale of housing on the open market to produce affordable rents

■ assist small black housing associations who might otherwise have found it difficult to develop in the area

Project Details
The Consortium included two well established associations, Leicester Housing Association and de Montfort Housing Society, and a developing Afro-Caribbean association named Foundation Housing Association.

Leicester City Council agreed to dispose of two sites to the Consortium.

The St Peters site was 4 acres in size and is located in an inner city area. It was purchased at the relatively low price of £140,000 per acre because of its previously stigmatised location and problematic land conditions. Prior to sale, the City Council demolished unpopular deck access blocks and cleared the land of all debris. The existing and surrounding infrastructure - in terms of roads, water, gas and electricity services - was adequate.

The Kirby Frith site was 40 acres in size, was located on the periphery of the city and included some land of prime private sector development potential. The City Council agreed to sell the site to the Consortium in tranches and the first parcel was purchased for £195,000 per acre.

The Housing Corporation gave a firm indication that HAG would be available for the purchase of each parcel of land as the development proceeded. This enabled the

Consortium to take a long term view of the potential to use profits from property sales to subsidise rents on rented units.

Originally, it was intended that the sale of homes at Kirby Frith would subsidise rented homes on both sites. However, the collapse of the property market reduced the value of the St Peters site and enabled the Consortium to buy it and to proceed with the scheme without any need for cross subsidy. The St Peters development will be completed in mid 1991 and rents have been held at an average of £160 per month. The 100 unit development includes a Category 2 sheltered scheme and, at the request of the City Council, specially designed larger homes to accommodate extended Asian households.

The Kirby Frith development will still be reliant on cross subsidy. The Consortium will develop around 175 homes for rent, 100 homes for shared ownership and 125 for outright ownership. The homes for shared ownership and outright ownership will be marketed by Consortium Homes Leicester Limited (see below) and all profits will be made available to subsidise the development costs of (and thus the rents charged for) the rented units. The means by which this will be achieved are explained below.

William Davis, a major local contractor, was competitively selected to construct the homes on the St Peters site and the first part of the Kirby Frith development. The Consortium decided to seek a 'design and build' scheme to keep costs (and thus rents) as low as possible.

The cross subsidy arrangements are simple in theory but, for legal reasons, complicated in practice.

The basic principles of cross subsidy, which are outlined in the chapter on 'Financial Assistance To Housing Associations', have been adhered to. The number of homes for sale has been restricted to the bare minimum required to provide the amount of cross subsidy needed. Local people in housing need will have the first option to buy.

No HAG is available for units for outright sale and limited HAG is available for units which are to be sold on a shared ownership basis.

The Consortium has decided to concentrate, initially, on developing the rented units. This will enable the Consortium to benefit from any up-turn in the property market. In other words, it may be easier to sell homes (at higher prices) at some time in the future than it is at present. Unfortunately, in the short term, Consortium members may have to use their own reserves to compensate for this deferment of cross subsidy.

Overcoming Legal Difficulties

To make the cross subsidy arrangements work, the Consortium had to overcome several hurdles imposed by charity law and government rules covering the payment of public subsidy.

To avoid the possibility of the cross subsidy being counted as a further public sector contribution (and leading to a corresponding reduction in HAG), the cross subsidy had to be received through gift or charitable donation from a body which is not registered with the Housing Corporation.

To maximise the cross subsidy, the Consortium had to minimise its tax liability.

The Consortium also wanted to develop a legal relationship between the (housing association) members of the Consortium, the City Council, the Housing Corporation and other housing associations who might wish to use the Consortium's development services.

The Consortium resolved these problems in the following way.

An Industrial and Provident Society named Leicester Social Housing Limited (LSHL) was created. Leicester Housing Association and de Montfort Housing Society and the City Council were each given two places on LSHL's management committee. Foundation Housing Association was offered one place on the committee.

LSHL was registered on H13 1977 Model Rules with the Registrar of Friendly Societies, which enabled it to enjoy the status of an 'exempt charity'. The main advantage of being an exempt charity is that the organisation does not have to register with, or submit annual accounts to, the Charity Commission but still obtains all the tax benefits associated with charitable status. The Society was registered with the National Federation of Housing Associations but not with the Housing Corporation.

An off-the-shelf trading company, whose objects included the purchase and sale of housing accommodation, was purchased by benefactors. The majority shareholding in the company was then transferred by gift to the ownership of LSHL. The trading company thus became as a 'wholly owned subsidiary' of the Society.

The trading company, which is known as Consortium Homes Leicester Ltd, will undertake the development of such land as is identified for sale, will generate 'profit' (not possible for an exempt charitable Industrial and Provident Society) and will execute a deed of covenant making over sums of money directly equivalent to that 'profit' to the LSHL. This will minimise the tax liability of the trading company and thus maximise the cross subsidy. The work commissioned by the company will be carried out, on an agency basis, by the housing associations involved in LSHL.

LSHL will then make interest-free loans to de Montfort Housing Society, Leicester Housing Association and Foundation Housing Association. In order to protect the charitable status of the loans, the loan agreements will target the use of the money towards elderly people and others 'in necessitous circumstances'. The money will be used to reduce the element of development costs which will be met through borrowing by around 15%, and will thus hold rents at affordable levels.

Each association will apply directly to the Housing Corporation for the HAG funding required to develop its share of rented units in the Consortium development.

Example

A land for nominations deal also involving Cross Subsidy
Sale of land by Leeds City Council to Leeds Partnership Homes

Background

The Leeds Partnership Homes (LPH) initiative represents what its partners believe to be the biggest social housing initiative ever developed in the United Kingdom. LPH is a partnership between Leeds City Council and five housing associations, supported by Housing Corporation funding, which will provide more than 1,800 new homes for rent and 300 new homes for sale in Leeds between 1991-4.

The partnership involves the City Council selling around 90% of its portfolio of housing land to LPH - a company set up to manage the scheme and facilitate the construction of new homes on the land. Sites for rented housing will be sold on to individual housing associations, as and when they are ready to develop them.

The City Council will also transfer a number of empty dwellings including 'cottage' flats, system built maisonette blocks, hard to let houses and other 'miscellaneous' pre-1919 properties. These are dwellings requiring improvement work which Leeds City Council cannot afford to carry out. The City Council will, however, retain some sites to generate future capital receipts for the provision of education and social services.

The City Council decided to sell the land because, at a time when it desperately needs to produce new homes, government-imposed financial restrictions have removed its ability to do so.

In 1989/90 Leeds City Council investigated 3,087 homeless cases and accepted 918 households as homeless. There are almost 20,000 households on the council's waiting list. There is also a major backlog of improvement work required to homes in Leeds (including the council's own stock) - in 1986 the DoE estimated that £600 million was needed for this task. Yet the council's Basic Credit Approval in 1990-1 was only £30 million - and this included 'assumed capital receipts' and money for urban renewal activity.

Within these constraints, and following representation from its tenants, the City Council recognised that its first priority must be the repair and improvement of its own stock and accordingly switched the emphasis of its capital programme away from new build.

The City Council calculated that the LPH initiative would give it access to around 25% more homes than if it sold land at market value and re-invested the useable receipt in direct new housing provision.

The activity of LPH will occur on up to 90 sites - both large and small - which extend throughout the metropolitan area of Leeds. This includes the pre-1919 terraced housing areas of the inner city, inter-war council estates and the ring of towns and villages around the old City of Leeds.

The Housing Associations taking part in LPH are Anchor, Leeds Federated, North British, the Ridings and Sanctuary. All five have operated in Leeds for some years - together they own about 4,500 homes in the city - and have worked closely with the City Council.

Each of the six partners has a seat on the Board of LPH. The Board is chaired by Councillor Alec Hudson, who is the City Council's representative and Chairman of the Council's Housing committee.

There are a number of housing associations which, while not full members of LPH, will work within its framework. These 'beneficiary associations' include Leeds Jewish Housing Association, St Anne's Housing Action, Unity Housing Association and Harewood Housing Society. LPH will also be working with Yorkshire Metropolitan Housing Association on specific schemes.

Objectives

The objectives of LPH are:

■ to provide affordable rented housing

■ to strengthen and extend the partnership between Leeds City Council and housing associations which operate in the city

■ to work with the private sector to produce profits which can be used to cross-subsidise rented housing

■ to use 100% of the value of the Council-owned land on social housing projects in Leeds

■ to 'stretch' the value of HAG and to maximise Leeds' share of available HAG

Sources Of Funding

The City Council's contribution to the initiative is the land, estimated value £33 million, which it is disposing at 'nil financial consideration' in return for nominations to the completed properties. The Council's legal and financial interest in the land will be protected by a detailed legal agreement which includes contractual commitments about the type of homes to be developed.

The land value (£33 million) will be matched by £33 million in HAG from the Housing Corporation. Housing associations will raise loans to cover the balance of development costs. It is hoped that private sector developers will invest similar amounts of money in the commercial development of those sites which have been earmarked for housing for sale.

'Land For Nominations' Arrangements

Leeds City Council will sell land and property to LPH at nil financial consideration in return for 75% nomination rights (falling to 50% after 20 years). Under the terms of Capital Finance Regulation 20(4), the City Council will not need to make provision to pay off outstanding debt. Following months of negotiation, the DoE has accepted the disposal of land and property to LPH by giving a specific direction under Section 61 (4) of the Act. In doing so, the DoE has accepted two key principles. First, that land can be transferred at less than market value in return for nominations through the conduit of a 'holding company' (LPH), which will pass on the nomination obligations to the individual associations which eventually purchase and develop the land. Second, that LPH can sell land transferred at nil financial consideration to private developers at full market value, provided that the sale proceeds are then used to stretch the HAG on those sites developed by housing associations.

Nominations have been valued by Leeds City Council at £24,000 a unit. The City Council calculated the value of each nomination by dividing the value of the land it was proposing to transfer (£33 million) by the total number of homes it would have access to under the LPH initiative - taking additional account of the fact that there would be no Right to Buy on the rented units developed under the LPH initiative. Leeds City Council took counsel's opinion to satisfy itself that it was acting within its powers. Details have been provided to the District Auditor.

How The Scheme Will Work

Leeds City Council will sell sites and empty properties to LPH at nil financial consideration.

LPH will, in turn, sell sites at nil financial consideration to housing associations. This will count as a public subsidy element and HAG (which must not exceed 67% of scheme costs on this project) will be reduced accordingly.

LPH will also sell some higher value sites to developers. This will produce significant profit to LPH as it purchased the sites for nil value. This will constitute a public finance subsidy towards the scheme which will again be used to reduce the

Leeds Partnership Homes initiative

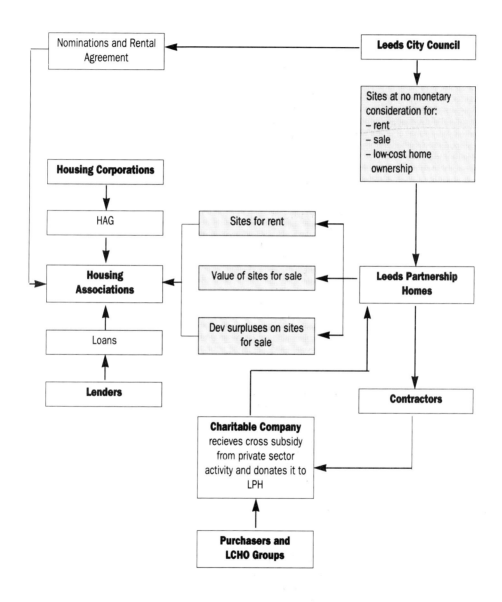

amount of HAG required.

Both these public subsidies will 'stretch' the HAG to other sites, allowing more than twice as many homes to be built than if the sites had been purchased at market value.

An important principle of the scheme is to ensure that rents for the new properties, whilst higher than those charged by the City Council itself, will still be 'affordable' to people on low incomes. Target rents will be set in agreement with the City Council and will be up-rated annually according to an agreed formula. However the ability of associations to meet these target rents will depend substantially upon the availability of 'top up' subsidy. This money will be raised by LPH in the following manner.

LPH will work with private sector developers to provide housing for sale. The profits from these private residential developments will be shared between LPH and the developer and LPH will use its share to cross-subsidise rented homes in order to make rents affordable. Alternatively, LPH will sell land to developers on a deferred purchase basis (thus reducing the developers risk and development interest costs) in return for a share in the developers eventual profit. Again, LPH will use any money obtained to cross subsidise rents.

If there is less 'top up' subsidy than expected, LPH's participant housing associations are not legally bound to charge the target rents.

Legal Agreements

The LPH programme is regulated by legal agreements:

■ General Acquisition Agreement - between Leeds City Council and LPH - commits LPH to certain activities, specifies the way in which LPH must manage the land sold to it and stipulates the tenure characteristics of the completed homes.

■ Specific Site Agreement - between the City Council and LPH - must be signed before each site is sold to LPH.

■ Agreement between LPH and individual housing associations for each site - before it is sold to the association - in which signed LPH passes on the obligations it has made to the council (under agreement b) to each association.

■ Nominations agreement - covering nominations and affordable rent levels (latter element subject to availability of 'topping up' funds).

■ Inter-association development agreement - an agreement covering working relationships and means of resolving disputes

■ Beneficiary agreement - covering the use and terms of transfer of completed units by LPH to Yorkshire Metropolitan Housing Association, Harewood Housing Society, Unity Housing Association and Leeds Jewish Housing Association.

Overcoming Legal Difficulties

As with the Leicester City Council example quoted above, the Leeds initiative has had to overcome legal and financial problems.

Leeds City Council could not have transferred land at less than market value to private developers without being caught by Section 61 of the Local Government and Housing Act . Nor, under the same debt redemption rules, could the City Council have passed on the full value of any private (cross) subsidy profits to housing associations. It was necessary to set up LPH, and for the City Council to sell the sites to LPH, to

Leeds Partnership Homes: Structure of the legal agreements

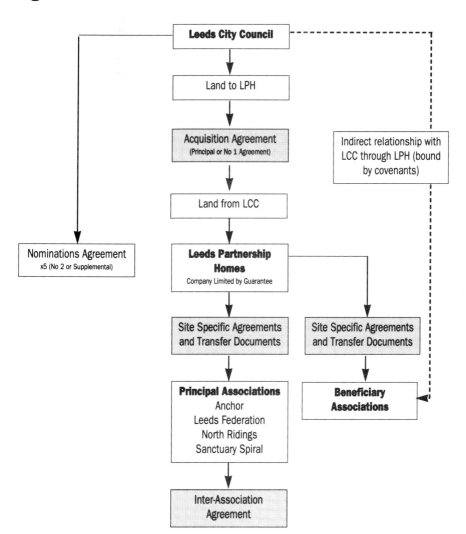

overcome this difficulty.

This in turn created a problem regarding the sale of land at less than market value in return for nominations to a body (LPH) which is not a registered housing association and thus not referred to in Regulation 20(4). Following DoE approval this problem has been resolved (see above).

In order to avoid paying tax on the 'top up' cross subsidy, this money has to be covenanted by LPH to a specially formed charitable company which will then make it available as a charitable donation to participant housing associations.

Progress So Far

At the time of writing, early May 1991, 18 sites have been sold to LPH by the City Council under an interim agreement. Of these sites, 17 will be developed for rent and 1 for low cost home ownership.

The low cost home ownership site involves the rehabilitation of former council houses and flats and the construction of 17 new homes and flats on shared ownership terms. The completed homes will be sold to first time buyers and other people nominated by the City Council.

2

FINANCIAL ASSISTANCE TO HOUSING ASSOCIATIONS

This chapter looks at the principal forms of financial assistance that local authorities can provide to housing associations which are seeking to develop new housing.
The chapter also looks at the possibility of introducing private sector subsidy, through a mechanism known as 'cross subsidy'.

Local Authority Housing Association Grant

Under Section 50 of the Housing Act 1988, the Housing Corporation is the sole source of Housing Association Grant (HAG). Local authorities can, however, 'sponsor' the capital costs of housing association projects on which the Housing Corporation pays HAG, under arrangements commonly known as 'local authority HAG'. These arrangements involve the local authority providing resource cover for all or part of the scheme costs. All forms of housing association development which are eligible for Housing Corporation HAG are also eligible for 'local authority HAG'.

'Local authority HAG' payments are not deducted from the Housing Corporation's overall approved development programme but are controlled under the Basic Credit Approval system, introduced by the Local Government and Housing Act 1989, for limiting local authority capital expenditure . HAG payments made by local authorities are re-imbursed by the Housing Corporation. The DoE is happy for this re-imbursement to take place because 100% of the money re-imbursed by the Housing Corporation must be set aside to cover the authority's existing debt. 'Local Authority HAG' is not available in Wales. For a brief discussion of arrangements in Wales see page 32.

How the system works

The local authority decides to provide funding for a housing association project, includes it in the formulation of its annual Capital Programme Bid to the DoE and informs the Housing Corporation of its intention to support the scheme. When the local authority receives confirmation of its approved capital programme from the DoE and confirms that it has sufficient resources to sponsor the scheme, the Corporation will respond by confirming the grant percentage to be applied, the grant limit for the scheme and the size of grant tranches to be paid.

The local authority will provide development loan funding to the housing association. On the day that payments are actually made, the local authority will receive an equivalent payment of Housing Association Grant to reimburse its expenditure. This is called 'back to back' funding and means that no actual cash outlay is required from the local authority.

The local authority can also provide a long term loan, where the association cannot

Local Authority HAG

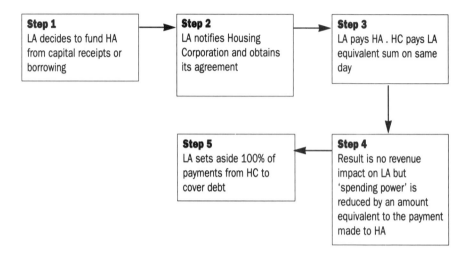

Step 1
LA decides to fund HA from capital receipts or borrowing

Step 2
LA notifies Housing Corporation and obtains its agreement

Step 3
LA pays HA . HC pays LA equivalent sum on same day

Step 5
LA sets aside 100% of payments from HC to cover debt

Step 4
Result is no revenue impact on LA but 'spending power' is reduced by an amount equivalent to the payment made to HA

obtain private finance, to 'top up' the 'local authority HAG' payment. However, long term loans are not reimbursed by the Housing Corporation.

Local authorities can fund associations from useable capital receipts, revenue funds or from borrowing sanctioned under their Basic Credit Approval (BCA).

Where 'borrowing power' is used, the level of assistance scores 100% against the authority's BCA credit limit.

Where the local authority uses capital receipts as the source of its subsidy, the receipts are replaced by the Housing Corporation but must then be 'set aside' to cover the authority's debt. They cannot be simply recycled as further capital expenditure, although interest obtained on the receipts can be channelled to housing associations in the form of grants under Section 24 of the Local Government Act 1988.

Capital funding of development costs cannot exceed the HAG rate which applies to Corporation funded schemes in the same region. The prevailing HAG rates are set out in Housing Corporation Circular 26/90. This limit on the amount of subsidy per scheme means that where further public subsidy is provided, the level of 'local authority HAG' must be reduced by a corresponding amount.

Local authorities wishing to make a long term commitment to housing associations may find it helpful to obtain their own Approved HAG Programme from the Housing Corporation. Where such a programme is agreed, the Corporation (under Section 50(4) of the Housing Act 1988) appoints the local authority as its agent for the assessment and payment of HAG. The authority does not have to submit individual schemes to the Corporation for checking and can thus save on admin costs and can progress schemes more quickly.

To be eligible for an Approved HAG Programme, local authorities must demonstrate a commitment to fund 20 schemes (of any size) in the next financial year and at least 16 and 10 schemes in the two subsequent years.

Advantages Of 'Local Authority HAG' For Local Authorities

New social housing is provided at minimal cost to the authority, because it is not saddled with loan repayments or costs associated with the management and maintenance of the property.

The 'back to back' funding arrangements create additional benefits. If the local authority planned to borrow money in order to fund housing association activity, the 'back to back' reimbursement of the borrowing by the Housing Corporation saves the authority from paying interest on that borrowing. If the authority planned to use capital receipts to assist housing associations, the 'back to back' reimbursement of this expenditure means that the receipt never actually leaves the local authority's bank account and (although it cannot then be recycled as further expenditure) the ability of those receipts to earn interest is maintained.

More new social housing can be provided than if the local authority developed the housing itself. This arises because, instead of meeting 100% of scheme costs, the local authority only provides funding equivalent to the prevailing HAG rate. Private finance meets the difference and is not deducted from the authority's credit limit. This will have greater impact in areas where the HAG rate is lower than the national average (75% of scheme costs) than in areas where the HAG rate is higher than the average. This advantage will not materialise where the local authority tops up the grant funding with a long term loan, as that would score against its credit limit.

The local authority may be able to secure better nomination arrangements than would be the case in mainstream HAG funded schemes. It is not uncommon for 'local authority HAG' funded schemes to attract 100% nomination rights.

It is the local authority who decides which schemes to fund. Thus it will be easier for the authority to persuade housing associations to meet its housing need priorities - such as providing accommodation for homeless households - than where the Housing Corporation is the primary funding agent.

Advantages Of 'Local Authority HAG' For Housing Associations

It provides an opportunity for associations to obtain HAG for projects which the Housing Corporation is unwilling or unable to fund.

The amount of 'local authority HAG' available to local authorities is neither cash limited nor deducted from the Housing Corporation's approved development programme, so payment of grant does not reduce the resources available to other associations.

Difficulties For Local Authorities

Typically, at least three extra staff are required to operate a minimum 'local authority HAG' programme. Unfortunately, administration costs (other than brokerage fees) are not reimbursed by the Housing Corporation. The authority can still, of course, levy these costs on the association. However, this would force the association to borrow more private finance and charge higher rents.

There is also likely to be competition for capital resources from elsewhere. For example, local authority tenants and housing management staff may feel that all available resources should be spent on the maintenance and modernisation of the authority's own stock. However, authorities may feel that the capital programme should contain a balance of improvement and new build schemes and should be able to demonstrate that housing associations are better placed to undertake new build at present.

Arrangements for 'Local Authority HAG' funding are described in detail in Housing Corporation Circulars 20/89 and 70/89, the Housing Corporation Local authority Schemework Procedure Guide.

Extent Of Local Authority Use Of 'LA HAG' Powers

The latest figures available from the Housing Corporation, for 1989-90, indicate that Local Authority HAG payments were used for 3,880 housing association homes for rent, 922 'miscellaneous works' to existing association properties (mainly major repairs to dwellings originally rehabilitated with local authority capital funding) and 313 homes for low cost sale.

Welsh Alternative To 'Local Authority HAG'

As stated above, 'Local Authority HAG' is not available in Wales. Instead the following arrangements apply. Readers will notice that they have an impact which is similar to 'Local Authority HAG'.

Where a local authority decides that it cannot use up all of its Basic Credit Approval loan sanction in the financial year to which it applies, it can 'redeem' the unused sum to Welsh Office. The Welsh Office is then able to convert the unused element of the 'loan sanction' into permission for Tai Cymru to make a cash grant to an association recommended by local authority.

Financial Assistance to Housing Associations under the terms of The Local Government Act 1988

The other common method of giving financial assistance is set out in the Local Government Act 1988 and covers revenue as well as capital funding.

Section 24 of the Local Government Act 1988 gives local authorities the power to provide financial assistance (grants, loans, sale of land at less than market value etc) for, or in connection with, housing that is privately let. This can be on the basis of a lease, a licence or a tenancy. Housing is privately let if the occupier's immediate landlord is not a local authority. The term thus covers housing developed by housing associations, private landlords and property developers. The financial assistance can be taken from the Housing Revenue Account or the General Fund.

The provision of financial assistance under this power is known as a 'gratuitous benefit' by the DoE and in most cases requires DoE consent under Section 25 of the Local Government Act 1988. (See Chapter on 'Sale Of Local Authority Land' for further discussion of Section 25).

However, the DoE has granted a general consent for financial assistance to shared ownership schemes (provided that the purchaser is taking out at least a 99 year lease and a minimum stake of 25% equity). The DoE has also granted a general consent enabling local authorities to provide financial assistance towards schemes providing rented housing, of up to £1 per head of population resident in their area under a general consent. This power can be used only once each financial year. Thus if there are 50,000 people living in a local authority area, a one-off grant of £50,000 can be made each year.

As with 'local authority HAG' any assistance given under Section 24 must not take the total level of public subsidy on a rental scheme above the Housing Corporation's HAG rate for a similar scheme in that area. The subsidy limit applies to any combination of HAG, local authority capital or revenue grant and the value of any discount on the value of the land sold or any other form of public subsidy. (See chapter on 'Sale Of Local Authority Land' for further discussion).

Private sector Cross Subsidy

Where public subsidy, from the local authority or the Housing Corporation, is either limited or unavailable, it may still be possible to develop social housing projects through subsidy from private developers.

Essentially, cross subsidy schemes involve developers making cash available or carrying out 'work in kind' in order to subsidise the costs of a social housing scheme. In return, the developer is normally given the chance to construct all the dwellings (thus obtaining 'contractor's profit') and is able to sell a proprortion of the completed homes on the open market (thus obtaining 'development profit').

In most cases, developers are unlikely to be interested in any scheme where they are asked to give up any of their normal 'operating' profit. However, developers may be more flexible if they are finding it difficult to acquire land in the area.

In most cases, developers will only be interested in cross subsidy if the scheme enables them to buy land at less than market value. In such cases the developer would make 'additional' profit and would be prepared to make over part of this additional profit as a 'quid pro quo'. Cheap land may become available under 'land for nominations' deals or under exceptional planning permission schemes (see chapters on 'Sale Of Local Authority Land' and 'Use Of Planning Powers').

The particular advantage of cross subsidy arrangements is that any benefit over and above that arising from a discount on the price of land sold by a local authority is classed as private subsidy and there is no corresponding reduction in HAG. (There are no specific DoE regulations regarding cross subsidy but the DoE has confirmed that this is how it treats cross subsidy 'in practice'.)

For example, where local authority land is sold at less than market value to a housing association, in return for nominations, the reduction in value is counted as public subsidy. However, if the association develops housing for sale (either itself or in concert with a developer) the proceeds of the sale housing count as private subsidy.

Cross subsidy arrangements need not involve a private developer at all. They can, as in the Leicester Consortium example (see chapter on 'Sale Of Local Authority Land'), involve a non-charitable arm of an existing association developing homes for sale. However, this type of arrangement will expose the housing association to additional risk - as has occurred in the Leicester example where the development of homes for market sale has been delayed pending an up-turn in the property market. In addition, housing associations may not have the entrepreneurial skills or knowledge of the private housing market to sell homes effectively.

Moreover, cross subsidy arrangements need not solely involve homes for outright owner occupation. It is possible to obtain financial benefit from shared ownership schemes if initial sale proceeds are greater than development costs. Clearly, however, more shared ownership units will be required than homes for outright occupation in order to generate the same amount of cross subsidy.

In order to preserve the integrity of a social housing scheme when employing cross-subsidy arrangements, two basic principles are generally observed. First, the number of homes for sale should be limited to the precise level required by the need for cross subsidy to help finance a particular project. Second, local people in housing need should have the first option to buy. This may produce the additional benefit of 'freeing up' tenanted units in the existing stock of the local authority or housing associations involved.

However, some local authorities have taken a more pragmatic approach. For example, in the Leeds Partnership Homes initiative (see chapter on 'Sale Of Local Authority Land'), Leeds City Council plans to transfer around half of its housing sites (via LPH) to private developers, without reference to the subsidy of any particular project, in order to maximise the capital receipt which can be channelled back into housing association development.

The range of cross subsidy arrangements are diverse as the range of local circumstances and the breadth of human ingenuity. (See the Leeds and Leicester examples discussed in Chapter 1).

Example

'Local Authority HAG' funding
The Royal Borough of Kensington and Chelsea

The Royal Borough of Kensington and Chelsea has provided 'local authority HAG' funding to housing associations operating within its boundaries since 1974. It has operated an 'LA HAG' Approved Development Programme since 1984. Partly as a result of this support, there are 12,000 housing association homes in the borough whereas the Borough's own stock numbers 8,000 units.

The Borough's 'LA Hag' programme averaged around £15 million in the late 1980's. However, due to a combination of increased restrictions on the use of its capital receipts and reduced borrowing approvals, the programme has fallen to £5 in 1990-91 and is likely to fall to around £4 million in 1991-92. At present, the Borough is supporting 13 of the 22 associations which are actively developing in its area.

This financial assistance has primarily taken the form of development loans although in half a dozen cases loan guarantees have been provided for shared ownership schemes or schemes which have been 100% privately financed. Since 'mixed funding' was introduced, no housing association has sought Borough assistance for the privately financed loan element of a scheme.

The nominations agreement between the Borough and local housing associations only specifies a nominations quota of 50% of true voids (see chapter on Nominations Agreements for details) but there is a distinct possibility that the Borough may seek a higher level of nominations in coming years.

The Borough has sought to maintain a balance between this support for housing association new build and the need to undertake repairs and improvements to its own housing stock. Consequently, its 1990-91 capital programme allows around £6 million for works to the Borough's own stock - slightly more than it gives to housing associations.

Example

'Local Authority HAG' funding
The London Borough Of Merton

The London Borough of Merton has provided a limited amount of 'local authority HAG' funding to local housing associations for several years, mainly to enable associations to undertake major repairs and re-improvements to stock initially developed using LB Merton or Greater London Council funds.

However, LB Merton has recently increased its provision of 'local authority HAG' considerably. In 1989-90 the 'local authority HAG' commitment was £800,000, in 1990-1 £3.1 million and in 1991-2 the amount rose dramatically to £6.5 million. The 1991-2 figure comprises over 50% of the borough's housing capital programme. The greater part of the 1991-2 allocation is funded through useable capital receipts with a smaller part originating from the borough's Basic Credit Approval borrowing power.

The increased 'local authority HAG' commitment in 1990-1 was largely intended to assist housing associations to undertake a programme of 'off-the-shelf' property acquisition. This represented an opportunistic response to the availability of cheaper property due to the downturn in the private housing market.

However, the further increase in 'local authority HAG' in 1991-2 represented a more developed housing strategy.

LB Merton, which changed political control from Conservative to Labour in 1990, was becoming increasingly anxious about its ability to meet local housing needs. Its housing waiting list had increased by 14% since 1985 and the number of households accepted as statutory homeless has risen from 213 in 1984-5 to an all time high of 335 in 1989-90. However, LB Merton was losing housing stock very quickly due to the Right To Buy. For instance, 48% of its houses had been purchased in this manner between 1980 and 1990. As a result, the number of applicants accommodated from the waiting list had declined from 250 in 1984/5 to 151 in 1989-90 and LB Merton feared that it would have to increase the amount of time that homeless households had to wait in temporary accommodation.

LB Merton decided that, to return to a position similar to 1985, it needed to gain access to 300 new homes over a period of three years. Unfortunately the debt redemption rules introduced by the DoE in 1990 meant that LB Merton would not be able to build that number of homes itself. Those that were built would still be at risk of loss to the Right To Buy.

LB Merton decided that the required number of homes could only be built by local housing associations. It decided to pursue a twin-track approach to assist associations in this task. First, it decided to sell 13 acres from its own land bank on a discounted basis in return for nomination rights. Second, as we have noted, it decided to double its 'local authority HAG' commitment. The money for this was found by abandoning (unpopular) plans made by the previous administration for highway improvement schemes and using the spending power intended for these schemes to provide new rented homes.

The principal advantages in this policy, as perceived by LB Merton, were that associations would build rented homes at less than LB Merton would have to pay to build them itself (due to access to private finance which the borough did not have) and that (due to back-to-back funding by the Housing Corporation) the expenditure would have no revenue impact on the General Fund.

At the time of writing, as a combined result of the sale of land at less than market value and 'local authority HAG' and Housing Corporation HAG funding, the construction of 348 new homes has been approved. Further schemes are in the pipeline which will carry the overall figure above 400 units.

The housing associations involved are Shaftesbury HA, London and Quadrant Housing Trust, Threshold HA, South London Family HA, Crystal Palace HA, Family HA, Wandle HA, Grenfell HA, Hanover HA and Merton Asian HA. The 20 flats which will be let to elderly Asian people by Merton Asian HA are being developed on their behalf by Hanover HA and represent MAHA's first scheme since its inception in October 1990.

Rents range from £50 to £55 per week for three bedroom houses and £44 to £47 for one bedroom flats, depending upon the site and association involved. Specific nomination agreements have been proposed for each site, although in most cases LB Merton is seeking 100% nominations on initial lettings.

The impact on the individual housing associations involved in the initiative is demonstrated by the experience of Wandle Housing Association.

At the time of LB Merton's decision to increase their provision of 'local authority HAG', Wandle HA was negotiating with the borough to purchase a site at Baker Lane and with agents acting for the Metropolitan Police to purchase 19 vacant homes on a site at Church Road. LB Merton indicated willingness to provide 'local authority HAG' funding and a discount on the price of the land for the purchase of the Baker Lane site, but were uncertain whether they had enough money to meet the full cost of the Church Lane acquisition. Wandle HA suggested that an approach be made to the Housing Corporation to see whether it would be prepared to 'top up' the 'local authority HAG' with HAG from its Approved Development Programme. The Housing Corporation agreed on the grounds that, by providing HAG equivalent to only 26% of overall scheme costs, 49 new units of rented housing would be developed.

Overall scheme costs were £4,832,000 and were met by LB Merton's combined contribution of HAG and land discount worth £2.2 million, Housing Corporation HAG of £1.3 million and a contribution of £1,312 from Wandle HA (part private loan and part use of existing reserves).

Wandle HA has offered LB Merton 100% nominations on initial lettings and, at the time of writing, this agreement is awaiting DoE approval.

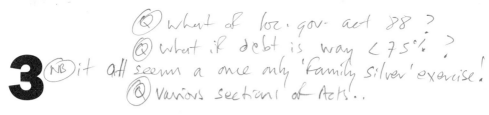

① what of loc. gov. act 88 ?
② what if debt is way < 75% ?
(NB) it all seem a once only 'family silver' exercise!
② various sections of Acts'..

3

TRANSFER OF LOCAL AUTHORITY HOUSING STOCK TO HOUSING ASSOCIATIONS

The purpose of this chapter is to explain how the transfer of local authority housing to housing associations can lead to:

■ more resources for the repair and improvement of that housing

■ more resources for the development of new housing

■ the protection of rented housing from purchase under the Right To Buy   9 4 w· pap ?

The chapter also explains:

■ the risks and difficulties associated with stock transfer

■ the need to obtain tenant approval to the transfer of occupied housing

Transfer can involve the whole of a local authority's housing stock and this is known as large scale voluntary transfer.

   Alternatively, it can involve particular estates or scattered properties and this is known as a partial (or selective) voluntary transfer.

   There are also special provisions for the transfer of housing stock which has been built or acquired for the specific purpose of resale or which has been designated as defective under the terms of Part 16 of the Housing Act 1985.   M E united + knightstone
among ?

Large Scale Voluntary Transfers

At the time of writing, (May 1991), the majority of large scale voluntary transfer proposals have involved local authorities transferring stock to newly created housing associations. However, there is no 'in principle' reason why large scale transfer should not take place to an existing housing association.

   The primary motivation for a large scale voluntary transfer is likely to be the authority's inability to meet local housing need due to diminishing capital resources. Voluntary transfer may be a means to release more capital funds, by effectively remortgaging the housing stock at the point of sale to a new landlord. Large scale transfers may be particularly attractive to local authorities which have a low outstanding loan debt in relation to the asset value of their housing stock. The local authority will be able to reinvest part of the capital receipt in the provision of new rented housing. (See below for further details).

   The other main advantages are as follows. Following transfer, new tenants will be able not be able to exercise the Right To Buy. This will mean that the loss of subsidised rented housing in the area is significantly reduced. The association which purchases the housing stock will also benefit from a significantly increased asset base. This will generate sufficient ability to borrow from private finance institutions to produce a substantial addition to number of low cost homes in the area.

Conversely, the housing association will take on an extremely large debt to purchase the property and will thus expose itself to a significant degree of financial risk. In particular, the ability of the association to repay this debt and to maintain rents at 'affordable' levels will depend largely on future trends with regard to a series of unpredictable factors including Right To Buy sales to transferring tenants, interest rates, rate of relets, unforseen structural defects and so on.

Readers who are interested in the pros and cons of large scale voluntary transfer may find it useful to read 'The Voluntary Transfer Of Local Authority Housing Stock' (ADC 1990), 'Voluntary Transfer: A Guide' (TPAS 1990) and 'Putting A Price On Council Housing: Valuing Voluntary Transfers' (Gardiner, Hills and Klienman - Welfare State Programme, LSE 1991).

At the time of writing, May 1991, 28 local authorities have proposed large scale voluntary transfers. Success has been dependent upon tenant approval (see below). In 16 cases a majority of tenants have supported the transfer and in 12 cases a majority of tenants have rejected the proposal.

Financial Considerations Arising From Large Scale Transfers

The Housing Corporation has made it clear that no Housing Association Grant (HAG) will be available to finance the transfer of or major repair or modernisation of

Transfer of Local Authority Housing Stock

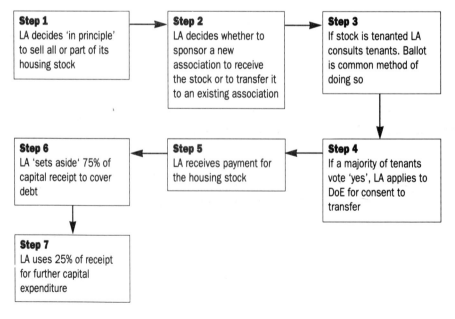

Step 1
LA decides 'in principle' to sell all or part of its housing stock

Step 2
LA decides whether to sponsor a new association to receive the stock or to transfer it to an existing association

Step 3
If stock is tenanted LA consults tenants. Ballot is common method of doing so

Step 6
LA 'sets aside' 75% of capital receipt to cover debt

Step 5
LA receives payment for the housing stock

Step 4
If a majority of tenants vote 'yes', LA applies to DoE for consent to transfer

Step 7
LA uses 25% of receipt for further capital expenditure

transferred property which is tenanted. HAG **is** available for the transfer of vacant housing.

Under DoE rules covering large scale voluntary transfers, 75% of the capital receipt must be 'reserved', that is set aside to cover debt. If the whole of the authority's housing and non housing debt would be cleared by less than 75% of the receipt, thus making the authority debt free, the residual sum may be spent (subject to restrictions explained below).

These rules mean that 25% of the capital receipt obtained from the sale of the housing stock is 'useable' for the purpose of reinvestment in social housing or, indeed, for any other purpose which the local authority may have in mind.

The local authority can employ the useable capital receipt to fund housing development by housing associations under Section 24 of the Local Government Act 1988 or via the 'Local Authority HAG' mechanism. (See chapter on 'Local Authority Financial Assistance To Housing Associations' for more details). The maximum subsidy per housing unit is limited to the standard HAG rate for that region, but this investment will normally attract further private sector finance.

DoE guidelines state that the spending of the 'useable capital receipt' obtained from the sale of housing must be phased over a period of years. Spending equivalent to £70 per community chargepayer in the local authority area is allowed in the year of transfer and spending up to £50 per chargepayer is permitted in subsequent years. Any underspend in one year can be carried over as a higher spend in the next year, but spending cannot exceed £70 per chargepayer in any individual year.

Where the residual receipt is concerned, DoE rules specifically state that the 'Local Authority HAG' mechanism cannot be applied and that any grants of this money must be made under Section 25 of the Local Government Act 1988. This means that if the residual receipt is used to fund social housing, it will disappear over time. However, the local authority can confine its assistance to interest earned on the residual receipt thus preventing the receipt itself from being eroded.

Partial Voluntary Transfers

Sometimes, a local authority will decide that it is prudent to propose the voluntary transfer of selected property.

As with large scale transfers, DoE rules stipulate that 25% of the capital receipt obtained can be re-invested in housing provision (or other capital expenditure) and the remaining 75% must be set aside to allow for the repayment of debt.

To date, several different approaches to partial voluntary transfer have been developed. For the sake of simplicity, we have divided them into three basic models.

The **first model** involves the transfer of tenanted estates 'en bloc'. This might take place where the cost of much needed repairs and improvements exceeds a local authority's financial resources or where the cost of these works would tie up a disproportionate amount of resources for a long time. In such situations, the transfer of the estate to an existing housing association (or to a newly formed tenant controlled landlord) may produce extra resources. The transfer would also leave the local authority better placed to spread its available capital resources more evenly amongst other estates which may have lesser, but still significant, repair and modernisation requirements.

Partial Voluntary Transfer: Models

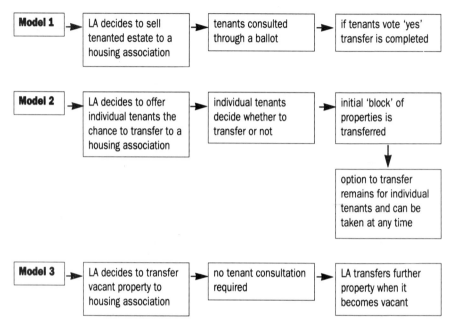

Extra resources for repairs to the transferred stock may be obtained as follows. In the pre-transfer valuation of the property, the cost of 'catch up' repairs is deducted from the assessed value. The term 'catch up' repairs primarily covers works which are required to remedy statutory nuisance or unfitness and which have not been carried out prior to transfer. The property thus becomes cheaper for a housing association to purchase and it can obtain mortgage finance which covers the cost of carrying out these works.

eh ?

Where the property is in an extremely bad condition, it may have a 'negative value' which will mean that a disposal cost or 'dowry' must be paid to the association. A disposal cost will occur where the cost of carrying out catch up repairs exceeds the value of the property when they have been carried out.

Where a disposal cost occurs, the money must be used by the purchasing housing association directly for the repair of the transferred property.

phase ratio

The local authority can pay the complete disposal cost at the time of transfer or, under certain circumstances, it can phase payment over a number of years. The DoE has agreed that the disposal cost can be phased if it is the equivalent of 7.5% or more of the local authority's capital expenditure on housing in the last financial year. If the disposal cost is between 7.5% and 15% of that figure, payment can be phased in equal instalments over two years. If the figure is 15% to 25%, payment can be phased over three years, if it is between 25% and 35% it can be phased over four years and, finally, if it is 35% or above it can be phased over the maximum period of five years.

Where the local authority has to meet a disposal cost, and proposes to pay it from within its Basic Credit Approval, the full extent of the cost will qualify for government subsidy. However, unless the DoE agrees to enhance the authority's Basic Credit Approval by an amount equivalent to the disposal cost, other capital expenditure will have to be met from revenue or slip to the following financial year. No government assistance is available for disposal costs paid from useable capital receipts obtained from other sales of land or property.

Extra resources for the modernisation and improvement of the transferred stock may be obtained as follows. The housing association acquiring the stock will be free from government spending constraints and (although no HAG can be paid on transferred tenanted housing) may be able to borrow sufficient money to undertake improvements. Where loan repayments on borrowing undertaken to finance improvements require rents to rise above affordable levels, vacant property can be sold by the association to reduce the borrowing requirement. Property sales of this nature are subject to DoE consent, which will only be granted as a 'last resort'.

The **second model** for partial transfer of stock involves the transfer of individual tenanted properties 'en bloc' or over a period of time. It allows the tenants of individual properties to opt for transfer to a housing association which will repair and modernise their homes more quickly than the local authority can. The DoE has indicated that it is willing to 'parcel up' individual properties into a 'block' for transfer consent purposes. It is anticipated that a 'dowry' will often be paid on the transferring stock in this type of transaction.

The **third model** involves the transfer of **empty** property to a housing association 'en bloc' or over a period of time. Again the likely local authority motivation is lack of resources to modernise and improve the property and the availability of such resources to a housing association. However, the local authority may also wish to maximise its useable capital receipt in order to finance works to its retained stock. This may lead, as in the Croydon transfer proposals, to the 'auctioning' of the stock to the housing association which is prepared to pay the highest price. Unless the purchasing association is able to provide further financial resources, from its reserves for example, this will lead to higher rents for new tenants occupying the transferred property. Unlike the transfer of tenanted property, no disposal cost or 'dowry' is payable on vacant property - although Housing Association Grant may be available.

Transfer of property built or acquired for resale

Local Authority Capital Finance Regulation (1990) Number 16 provides incentives to local authorities to build or convert houses or flats for subsequent sale to housing associations or to buy (and where appropriate improve) houses or flats for subsequent sale to housing associations.

The regulation does this by allowing the authority to deduct certain expenditure related to these activities from the capital receipt obtained from the sale, thus leaving a smaller capital receipt from which 75% has to be set aside for debt redemption. (For a more detailed discussion of the advantages to be obtained from this type of deduction, see chapter on 'Sale Of Local Authority Land').

The precise terms of Regulation 16 are as follows.

Under Regulation 16, when authorities build or convert houses or flats and sell them without first letting them on secure tenancies, they are able to offset the building or conversion or improvement costs against the sale proceeds before they apply the debt redemption rules. If building work takes place on land bought by the authority within three years of the sale it is also able to offset the cost of the land.

Similarly, when authorities buy houses or flats and sell them on without first letting them on secure tenancies, they are able to offset the cost of acquisition against the receipts. In such cases of 'purchase for resale' no time limits apply.

When authorities sell houses or other buildings they are able to offset against the sale proceeds any money they have spent on improvements to the property in the year of sale or the two previous financial years.

Transfer of stock which has been designated as defective

Under Part 16 of the Housing Act 1985, a local authority has a statutory obligation to ex-tenants who purchased defective dwellings from it:

■ to repurchase their home (paying up to 95% of the defect free value of the property), and

■ to carry out works to re-instate the dwelling to a condition where it is fit for habitation, or

■ to provide alternative accommodation where such works are impractical

The Local Authority (Capital Finance) Regulations (1990) provide an incentive for local authorities who are in this position to sell those dwellings and to use consideration received to pay for works to retained defective dwellings or to pay for the replacement of defective dwellings which cannot be adequately repaired. Regulation 18 does this by allowing the authority to deduct certain expenditure related to these activities from the capital receipt obtained from the sale, leaving a smaller residual receipt from which 75% has to be set aside for debt redemption.

Where the capital receipt is obtained in the form of money, the local authority can offset the total cost of any of the following types of expenditure which are incurred in the scheme:

■ the cost of newly acquired land

■ works to any building on existing local authority or newly acquired land

■ the cost of replacing any building on existing local authority or newly acquired land

provided that:

■ the costs of the land and/or rebuilding or conversion are broadly equal to the reasonable cost of an equivalent replacement of the former building.

■ the decision to dispose of the land is made not more than 3 years before the disposal or receiving of receipts.

The whole of the consideration received from the disposal can take the form of replacement land or the construction of or works to a building. Where capital receipts take the form of non-monetary consideration the deduction is determined by reference to the value of land and/or buildings received.

Secretary of State consent and tenant consultation

abv. and below ? consid's/restrics.

The consent of the Secretary of State for the Environment is normally required for the sale of local authority housing. The only exceptions concern property which has been built/acquired for resale or has been designated as defective. A general consent for these types of stock transfer has been issued by the DoE.

The Secretary of State will have regard to tenant views when considering whether to give consent to the transfer of **tenanted stock**. Consent will not be granted if a majority of the tenants affected by the transfer are opposed to it. In effect, therefore, transfers of tenanted stock cannot take place without tenant consent. Although there is no statutory requirement to do so, local authorities have generally perceived the advantages of holding a formal ballot of tenants to ascertain tenant views.

In most cases, the independent Electoral Reform Society has been employed to conduct the ballot and act as an independent teller.

Experience of large scale transfers indicates that tenants are as likely to vote 'against' a transfer proposal as 'for' it. At the time of writing (May 1991), tenants have voted in support of transfer in 16 cases and against transfer in 12 cases. In several other instances, transfer proposals have been withdrawn prior to a ballot due to the extent of tenant opposition. As transfer initiatives involve considerable expense and staff time and because rejection of transfer may lead to a breakdown of tenant confidence in their landlord, local authorities will naturally wish to take action to minimise the possibility of a majority 'no' vote. Some authorities have spent large sums of money on expensive public relations exercises but these have often proved to be counter-productive. Tenants have become suspicious of 'hard sell' techniques which are not accompanied by an open debate on the proposals.

Experience has shown, instead, that it is important to involve tenant representatives in the decision making process as early as possible, to reach agreement with these representatives on whether transfer is necessary and to pay for tenants (as a whole) to obtain independent advice on the transfer proposal before they vote. The Association of District Councils and the Tenant Participation Advisory Service (TPAS) have both published guidance on these matters.

Perspective of Housing Associations purchasing transferred stock

From a housing association perspective, stock acquisition is a major undertaking.

Where large scale voluntary transfers are concerned, the newly created housing associations which have been formed to acquire the property may be better placed than the local authority to repair, modernise and add to the housing stock. The pros and cons are discussed, briefly, above. However, the fact that tenants have rejected large scale transfers in 12 of the 28 ballots so far indicates significant debate as to whether a new landlord will be better placed to provide affordable social housing.

or in just the fact that suspicion outweighs poss. benifits

Most partial voluntary transfers will take place to existing housing associations, for whom the benefits are fairly clear.

The association can ameliorate local housing problems and enlarge its asset base at the same time. The acquisition of stock may also cement the working relationship between the association and the local authority concerned. This may, in turn, lead to future development opportunities for the association in that local authority area.

Synergy

However, difficulties must also be acknowledged.

Unless structural surveys are very rigorous, the association may be taking on responsibility for unforseen and costly structural defects. *can action in retrospect be taken*

The association may be unused to managing estate property, for example, and may quickly have to become expert at a range of functions such as environmental improvement, civil engineering and the legal issues surrounding the Right To Buy. In addition, tenants may have unrealistic expectations about the speed of repairs and improvements and changes in the nature of housing management.

Most important, it is essential that the valuation of the stock accurately reflects the real future costs of owning, managing and repairing it. Failure to do so may again place the association at undue financial risk. As we have noted, valuation involves assumptions about unpredictable variables such as movements in interest rates, management and maintenance costs, rate of relets and Right to Buy sales.

Perspective of Local Authorities which have transferred all their housing stock

Where an authority disposes of its entire housing stock it will not divest itself of all its housing responsibilities or the need to undertake housing-related activity.

The authority will retain its statutory responsibility under Part 3 of the Housing Act 1985 to secure housing for homeless households. The current code of guidance related to these responsibilities reminds authorities that they "cannot delegate the assessment of a homeless case to the purchaser to whom the stock is transferred".

The authority will therefore need to continue to employ housing staff to undertake the assessment of applications for housing by homeless people. It may also wish to provide temporary accommodation for applicants whilst their claims are being assessed. Where large scale transfers have taken place it is normal, as part of a nominations agreement, for the purchasing housing association to rehouse homeless people to whom the authority accepts a statutory obligation. Clearly, the authority will need to employ staff to ensure that the terms of this agreement are met, particularly with regard to the speed at which rehousing is offered, and to participate in future reviews or renegotiation of the agreement.

LA HAs ?

The local authority may also wish to assist the purchasing association (and other housing associations operating in the area) in future development. Discussions will need to take place regarding the level of this funding and the nature of the projects to which the money should be applied.

The local authority may also seek the involvement of retained housing staff in terms of the planning, housing benefit and special needs liaison with associations discussed elsewhere in this publication.

Example

A large scale stock transfer

Ryedale District Council And Ryedale Housing Association

In February 1991, Ryedale District Council in North Yorkshire transferred its entire housing stock to the newly created Ryedale Housing Association. This followed a tenant ballot in which 83% of the Ryedale DC tenants who voted supported the transfer proposal.

The Council was faced with a repairs backlog costing an estimated £6.01 million, together with the need to undertake planned maintenance and upgrading work. To meet these requirements Ryedale Council estimated that it would need to spend £1.9 million per year for the next 8 years. Under the new financial regime for local authority housing, introduced by the Local Government and Housing Act 1989, this would have required rent rises of 'inflation plus 35%' between 1990 and 1993.

Ryedale Council estimated that it needed to build a minimum of 20 new homes per year in order to meet its statutory obligations to rehouse homeless households. After the useable proportion of capital receipts obtained from Right To Buy sales had been spent, the bulk of this expenditure would have had to be met from rent revenue. This would have required a further rent rise of 24% between 1990 and 1993.

Ryedale Council did not believe that tenants could afford rent rises of 'inflation plus 59%' and did not expect its overall capital position to improve in the foreseeable future.

Ryedale Council was also concerned about the loss of stock through the Right To Buy. On 1st April 1989, its stock numbered 3498 units of which only some 1300 were statutorily protected from the Right To Buy. The Council had lost 1195 homes since the Right To Buy was introduced in 1980. Future sales were projected at 50 to 55 per year initially, decreasing over time. If the stock was transferred, however, an increasing number of properties (relets and new build) would be protected as new tenants would not be eligible to exercise the Right To Buy.

For these reasons Ryedale District Council proposed the transfer of its entire housing stock to Ryedale Housing Association, which it sponsored specially for this purpose.

Ryedale District Council agreed to meet the cost of independent advisers chosen by tenants. Tenants interviewed three firms at a public meeting and chose the Tenant Participation Advisory Service (TPAS). Using the advice provided by TPAS, the tenants steering group negotiated improvements to the tenancy agreement on offer and secured an increase of £50 per unit per year in future expenditure on planned maintenance and major repairs. On this basis, the tenants steering group felt able to recommend acceptance of the transfer proposals to all tenants voting in the ballot.

Under the transfer rules explained above, the cost of catch up repairs was deducted from the valuation and these repairs will be carried out over five years at no extra cost to tenants.

The stock was valued at £28.286 million which produced a useable capital receipt of £7. The Council proposes to use this receipt as the basis of 'Local Authority HAG' funding to the association over the next 5 years. The maximum subsidy per housing unit is 69% of costs – equivalent to the local Housing Association Grant rate. When private finance is attracted to meet the remaining 31% of costs, this will produce a development programme of 236 units over the first five years of Ryedale Housing Association's existence. The 'useable receipt' of £7 million will not diminish in size, because under 'Local Authority HAG' rules the expenditure is re-imbursed by the Housing Corporation. However, as 'Local Authority HAG' payments from the Housing Corporation cannot simply be recycled as further capital expenditure, the 'spending power' of the useable receipt will have been largely exhausted after year 5 (1991-1966). (See chapter on 'Financial Assistance To Housing Associations for further discussion). At this point, Ryedale DC plans to switch the nature of its assistance to annual grants paid under Section 24 of the Local Government Act 1988. The source of funds for these grants will be interest earned on the 'useable receipt' and the 'residual receipt' of £2.2 million which was left after money had been set aside to cover Ryedale DC's historic debt.

Following transfer, a legal agreement was drawn up between Ryedale District Council and Ryedale Housing Association regarding procedures for dealing with homeless households. It was agreed that Ryedale Housing Association will investigate applications for housing made by homeless people and will provide temporary accommodation while their application is being assessed. In accordance with its legal responsibility, and on the basis of a report from the association, Ryedale District Council will then decide whether there is a statutory duty to rehouse that household. If the District Council decides that a statutory duty does exist, Ryedale Housing Association will allocate the household a permanent home.

Example

A partial stock transfer
Knowsley Metropolitan Borough Council
and Local Housing Associations

Over 700 vacant 'walk up' flats and maisonettes in Kirkby owned by Knowsley MBC are being converted into houses and bungalows as part of a programme of stock transfer to local housing associations employing Housing Corporation 'special initiatives' funding.

The initiative arose from a research study conducted by Knowsley MBC which indicated that an increasing numbers of homes were becoming vacant and hard to let as a result of a depopulation of the area. Similar problems have been observed in the Knowsley MBC area as a whole. There was particular concern that the projected exodus was most marked amongst families in the 15 - 44 age group (the most likely child-producing group), which threatened to intensify the depopulation of the area.

Maintaining and increasing the local population was seen as a key objective by Knowsley MBC if an increasingly blighted local environment was to be avoided. The borough acknowledged that an alteration to the amount and type of the local rented housing stock was required, with as little additional urban blight as possible, if the population was to be retained.

The borough recognised that building a lot of new homes was not the solution, as it would inevitably add to the large number of derelict sites in the area. However, selective new build, on existing derelict sites and with the intention of ensuring the most appropriate dwelling mix, will form part of the initiative.

The strategy is designed to run for 5 years, during which it is hoped that the local housing stock will be reduced by 1,200 units and that 422 new dwellings will result from conversions. Maisonettes will be converted into traditional houses and three storey 'walk up' flats into bungalows. Works will cost, on average, around £55,000 per dwelling.

The Housing Corporation made it clear that HAG would be available to fund these works, but only if the properties were vacant at the time of transfer. In order to obtain HAG, Knowsley MBC has decided the properties will be decanted (with rigorous consultation with local residents) prior to transfer.

Knowsley MBC took the decision to transfer stock because it was unable to undertake its area improvement strategy due to government - imposed spending restrictions. Indeed, its Basic Credit Approval of £6.4 million in 1991-2 was only sufficient to fund basic work (such as rewiring), structural repairs and improvements to system built properties in other parts of the borough. Stock transfer, to local housing associations, provided the means by which additional financial resources could be provided. Although the stock to be transferred has been reasonably well maintained, dwellings are being sold at an average price of around only £2000 per property.

At the time of writing (May 1991), the first scheme under the strategy, involving the conversion of flats into houses and bungalows by Liver Housing Association, has already begun. The Housing Corporation has also guaranteed funding for four other schemes of similar character involving Liver Housing Association, Co-operative Development Services (CDS) and Merseyside Improved Homes. Two of the schemes will be managed by housing co-operatives. Liverpool Housing Trust will also be involved at a later date. HAG levels of 79% of scheme costs have been agreed by the Housing Corporation.

The associations have agreed, and the DoE has approved, that 100% nomination rights to the new homes will be available to Knowsley MBC. Rents on the new homes will not initially exceed £40 per week.

As a result of the endorsement of the Kirkby Strategy by the Housing Corporation and the Merseyside Task Force, Estate Action resources of £1.75 million have been agreed by the DoE for improvements to council-owned 'No Fines' housing in the Kirkby area which is not being transferred to housing associations. These works will ensure an overall improvement to all dwellings on the Kirkby estates.

Example

Hypothetical use of Regulation 18 to replace defective housing

The local authority might undertake such action in the following manner.

Step 1
Local authority sells part (Part A) of a rundown low density estate to a housing association.

Step 2
The housing association demolishes Part A of the estate and redevelops it for rental or 'for sale' housing (for outright or shared ownership).

Step 3

The local authority uses the capital receipt obtained from the housing association to replace defective dwellings on Part B of the estate.

In normal circumstances, the local authority would have to set aside 75% of the capital receipts obtained upon the disposal of Part A of the estate. However, because defective housing is being replaced, the authority can offset the cost of demolition and rebuilding under Step 3.

4

USE OF LOCAL AUTHORITY PLANNING POWERS

One of the key functions of the planning system is to provide an adequate and continuous supply of land for housing development in the right location and at appropriate standards.

The purpose of this chapter is to explain how local authorities can use their planning powers to:

■ help make privately owned land available to housing associations for social housing

■ (indirectly) help reduce the value of this land

Land costs normally represent between 25% and 50% of overall development costs. Reduced land costs will:

■ save on public subsidy to housing associations

■ produce cheaper housing costs for tenants or shared owners

■ enable development to take place, in some cases, even if no Housing Corporation funding is available

How the planning system works

County councils prepare structure plans which state broad planning policies for their county, within the context of regional guidance issued by the Secretary of State for the Environment.

District councils prepare local plans which, within the framework of the structure plan, identify specific sites and allocate their use for the next ten years. To date, not all the country is yet covered by detailed local plans.

The structure plan outlines the number of homes that need to be built in the county on a district-by-district basis but the actual allocation of sites for housing takes place in the local plan. Other sites are normally allocated for agricultural, commercial or industrial development.

Sites are allocated for housing on a 'general needs' basis. The allocation process is not, normally, permitted to distinguish between developer or tenure type.

In exceptional circumstances, however, councils may be prepared to agree to housing development on land which was not allocated for housing in their local plan.

In metropolitan districts, this two-tier approach does not apply. Instead, the local authority draws up a unitary development plan which incorporates most of the features of structure and local plans.

How planners can help make cheap land available

There are four main methods - which can be applied individually or together:

■ Amending local plans to state that the willingness of developers to provide social housing will be treated as a material planning condition when applications for planning permission are being considered.

■ Amending site planning briefs (often known as 'development briefs') which planners draw up for individual sites, to require the provision of an amount of social housing in any development of that site.

■ Negotiating planning agreements with developers and housing associations to ensure their compliance with the 'social housing' requirements of the structure and local plans and the planning brief.

■ Granting exceptional planning permission for social housing projects on land which has not been allocated for general needs housing.

Local Plan Policies For Affordable Housing

Government policy on this issue is outlined in DoE Circular 7/91, which states that:

■ A community's need for affordable housing may be taken into account when formulating local plan policies

■ New housing developments of a substantial scale should incorporate a reasonable mix and balance of house types and sizes to cater for a range of housing needs

■ Where there is a lack of low cost housing to meet local needs, planning authorities may reasonably seek to negotiate with developers for the inclusion of an element of affordable housing in such schemes, and may include policies in local plans indicating their intention to do so. Such policies should give clear guidance on what the authority would regard as affordable housing and on what arrangements they would expect to be made to ensure that such housing is reserved for those who need it

■ Local plan policies should not be expressed in favour of any particular form of tenure

■ Where there is such a policy in the local plan, the willingness of a developer to include an element of affordable housing on land allocated for residential use will be a material consideration which the planning authority should take into account in considering the application (for planning permission)

■ The precise amount of low cost housing should be a matter for negotiation with the developer. Planning policies which seek to impose a fixed quota on developers - for example that every development will include a set amount of social housing - will not be upheld by the Secretary of State for the Environment should the developer lodge an appeal

Amending Site Planning Briefs

It is normal for planning briefs to make stipulations regarding design, density, infrastructure or environmental factors but the brief can also include the requirement to provide a certain amount or type of social housing.

The amendment of planning briefs, to require the provision of an amount of social housing in any development of that site, is best undertaken when the local plan is being reviewed.

Planning Agreements

Planning agreements are commonly known as Section 52 agreements as they were originally sanctioned by Section 52 of the Town And Country Planning Act 1971. However, all planning legislation has now been consolidated into the Town And Country Planning Act 1990. Planning agreements are covered by Section 106 of that Act.

Under Section 106, planning authorities can enter into agreements with:

'any person interested in land in their area for the purpose of restricting or regulating the use of land . . . and any such agreement may contain such incidental and consequential provisions (including provisions of a financial character) as appear . . . necessary or expedient.'

These type of agreements are often known as 'planning gain'.

When landowners and developers are seeking planning permission, planning authorities can negotiate an agreement whereby the developer agrees to sell a number of homes cheaply to a housing association or to sell part of the site cheaply to a housing association. The developer would normally use cross subsidy from profits generated from market sale housing to finance this package.

Government policy on planning agreements which deal with social housing is stated in DoE Circular 7/91:

■ The element of affordable housing to be provided must be freely negotiated with the developer. A fixed quota should not be required

■ The planning agreement can restrict the occupation of the low cost housing to people falling within particular categories of need, provided that the criteria are specified in the local plan

■ Planning agreements cannot normally be used to impose restrictions on tenure, price and ownership. The authority will need to employ other mechanisms to deal with these matters. (In practice, restrictive covenants imposed by the vendor binding the future use of the land are the common means of achieving this)

■ The authority should also ensure that the benefit of affordable housing will be enjoyed by successive as well as initial occupiers of the property. The best way of achieving this is to involve a housing association or other social body (such as a trust) in the provision of housing for rent or shared ownership; its continuing interest in the property will ensure control over subsequent changes of ownership and occupation

Exceptional Planning Permission Scheme

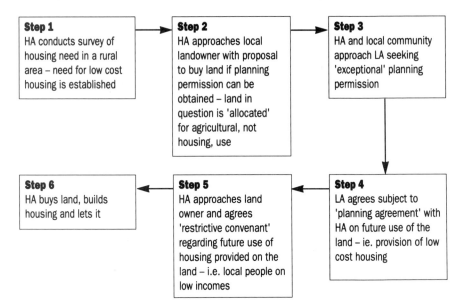

Step 1
HA conducts survey of housing need in a rural area – need for low cost housing is established

Step 2
HA approaches local landowner with proposal to buy land if planning permission can be obtained – land in question is 'allocated' for agricultural, not housing, use

Step 3
HA and local community approach LA seeking 'exceptional' planning permission

Step 4
LA agrees subject to 'planning agreement' with HA on future use of the land – ie. provision of low cost housing

Step 5
HA approaches land owner and agrees 'restrictive convenant' regarding future use of housing provided on the land – i.e. local people on low incomes

Step 6
HA buys land, builds housing and lets it

Exceptional Planning Permission Schemes

Planning agreements also play a part in exceptional planning permission schemes - sometimes known as 'off plan' schemes - which work as follows.

■ The allocation of land for general needs housing will generally inflate its development value. In many areas, it is difficult for housing associations to produce affordable housing on general needs housing land.

■ But by granting 'exceptional planning permission' on sites which have not been allocated for general needs housing - where the development value is not therefore inflated - local authorities can help housing associations buy land which is less expensive.

Government policy on exceptional planning permission schemes in rural areas is expressed as follows in DoE Circular 7/91:

■ These schemes may be relevant with regard to the release of small sites, within or adjoining existing villages, which would not otherwise be allocated for housing

■ The sites should not be formally allocated in the local plan but should be made available on a genuinely 'exceptional' basis

■ Land allocated for general needs housing cannot be reserved, through the use of planning mechanisms, for low cost housing for local people

■ Low cost housing provided as a result of an exceptional planning permission scheme should be retained as social housing in perpetuity

■ Whilst planning authorities can devise their own definitions of local housing need, it is expected that 'priority needs' groups will include existing residents who need self contained housing, people who provide important services and need to live closer to the local community, people who are not resident locally but have long standing links with the local community and people who need housing in order to take up a job offer in the area

■ Whilst the general presumption against development in the Green Belt is unaltered, exceptional planning permission schemes may be considered in some of the more extensive areas of Green Belt away from the urban fringe or within existing settlements which fall inside the Green Belt

Most of the exceptional planning permission schemes which have been approved so far have been developed in rural areas - many as the result of Rural Housing Trust initiatives.

Most of the suitable sites will be found on agricultural land. The effect of planning approval for a low cost housing development on this land will be to raise its development value from between £700 to £2,000 per acre to around £10,000 to £15,000 per acre. This will make it more likely that the landowner will put it on the market - thus enabling a housing association to develop it for low cost housing. As the market value for land allocated for general needs housing in rural areas ranges from £200,000 to £500,000 per acre, the savings produced are self evident.

In urban areas where land values are high, land which has not been allocated for housing may still command a high price. Non-housing land will have commercial development potential and owners will expect a higher price than might be obtained for rural land allocated for agricultural use. The scope for releasing 'very cheap' land through 'exceptional planning permission' may therefore be limited.

Nevertheless, there may still be sufficient difference between the value of housing and non-housing land to make the exercise worthwhile in urban areas. Contrary to popular opinion, there is no DoE objection to 'exceptional planning permission' in urban areas.

Social housing must be retained in perpetuity in exceptional planning permission schemes

This DoE requirement presents no difficulty where an association seeks to develop housing for rent.

However, problems arise on HAG-funded shared ownership schemes where the occupier eventually purchases 100% of the equity and then sells the property on the open market. As any subsequent owner will have to purchase 100% of the equity outright, the property is no longer available as low cost social housing.

One solution to this problem is to restrict the ability of a shared owner to acquire 100% of the equity of a dwelling.

In DoE Circular 7/91, the government states that public subsidy for housing association and other shared ownership schemes in rural settlements of less than 3,000 population will **not** be conditional on the shared owner having a right to staircase to full ownership. But to avoid the problem of shared owners being unable to move on to full ownership of another dwelling, because they own insufficient equity to be able to do so, the limit on staircasing should be set as high as possible - normally at least 80% of the value of the property. (The right of owners to staircase to full ownership will continue to be a pre-condition of public subsidy in all other circumstances).

The Housing Corporation has announced in Circular 34/90 that HAG funding will be available to enable housing associations, if they wish, to repurchase shared ownership properties in rural areas and to re-sell them on a shared ownership basis. This policy originated in Wales, in Tai Cymru Circular 4/89.

Cross Subsidy Arrangements

In most exceptional planning permission schemes, registered housing associations or village trusts have provided homes for rent or shared ownership, often with the aid of public subsidy (such as HAG). Where private sector agencies have been involved it has primarily been in the role of the building contractor.

However, because only a limited amount of public subsidy is available, some authorities have supported schemes which involve private developers in an enhanced role.

This type of scheme normally involves the developer acting as joint co-ordinator of the project, building a number of homes for outright sale on the open market and using the proceeds to subsidise the sale of rented and shared ownership units to a local housing association. (See chapter on 'Financial Assistance For Housing Associations' for a more detailed discussion of cross subsidy).

The involvement of private developers in exceptional planning permission schemes has been subject to much debate. The Rural Housing Trust, for instance, opposes their involvement on the grounds that local people are less likely to support schemes which involve developers and that landowners may seek higher prices for their land which will make the schemes unworkable. Other agencies such as ACRE have argued that without this type of cross subsidy arrangement, there may be too few schemes to meet housing demand.

DoE Circular 7/91, however, states that the government does not consider that any exceptional planning permission scheme should include 'high value' housing even if the purpose is to cross subsidise the social housing.

Instead, the Circular suggests that affordable housing in exceptional planning permission schemes could be cross subsidised by private sector profit generated from separate developments which take place on land allocated for general needs housing.

The need for a more radical approach?

Government policy of reliance upon the use of planning agreements with developers and exceptional planning permission schemes has been criticised by the Council For The Protection of Rural England (CPRE) and Communities and Homes In Central London (CHICL) on the ground that this approach will not stimulate sufficient social housing development to meet demand.

CPRE and CHICL have also criticised exceptional planning permission schemes on the ground that they:

"will encourage housing development in the most environmentally sensitive locations...precisely the areas where planning permission would not normally be available. The sensitive boundary between England's villages and the countryside, which has been officially protected for decades, is where the new development is being officially steered."

Instead, CPRE and CHICL have suggested the introduction of a new 'social use class' for housing. CPRE and CHICL point out that existing 'use class' arrangements allow local authorities, when giving planning permission or allocating land in the local plan, to specify whether a site can be used for shops, offices, food and drink, industrial, agricultural or residential development. The CPRE and CHICL proposal would extend this principle and allow authorities to earmark a proportion of the land they allocate for housing development to meet the needs of people who cannot afford to buy housing on the open market, and to grant separate planning permissions for 'general needs' or 'social' housing.

CPRE and CHICL contend that this approach would reduce the price of land allocated for 'social housing' and would thus yield more low cost land for social housing development. This approach would also give planning authorities more strategic control over the type of sites allocated for housing development.

Critics of the 'social use class' proposals, including the DoE, have said that:

■ It could lead to the creation of exclusively low-cost housing areas where other types of development are excluded.

■ That it would be almost impossible to maintain low cost housing developed for outright ownership as low cost housing in perpetuity - therefore it might be prudent to solely develop rented or shared ownership housing under such initiatives.

■ It would be difficult for councils to establish objective criteria for the division of land allocated for housing into (higher value) general needs and (lower value) social housing zones.

■ If the land allocated for social housing had previously been allocated for general needs housing, its owner could claim compensation under Section 17 of the Land Compensation Act 1961 for any loss in value which arose from its re-allocation

However, it is very unlikely that 'exceptional planning permission schemes' will produce anything like the required amount of social housing. Nor, given the vagaries of the market and the differing attitudes of private developers, can it be assumed that sufficient social housing will be produced through planning agreements with developers.

A more substantial change in the relationship between the planning system and housing development is required, with local authority housing and planning departments playing a joint 'enabling' role.

The present approach of allocating land solely for general needs housing is inadequate in terms of meeting public housing needs which (as Association Of District Councils research has demonstrated) include market housing for sale, shared ownership housing for sale, social housing for rent and market housing for rent.

As they presently stand, the Use Class Order proposals may not be practical. However, it may well be possible to improve and develop these proposals.

For instance, rather than allocating one vacant site for general needs housing and another for social housing, planners could allocate part of every large site for social housing. This could be done on a quota basis, with perhaps 20% of each site being allocated for social housing. In this way, individual landowners would not suffer arbitrary treatment and local authorities could be assured that a certain amount of social housing would be provided.

However, a change of DoE policy would be required to enable local authorities to impose this type of fixed quota. And the quota could only be imposed on previously unallocated land or when the local plan is reviewed. Any change to land allocated for general needs housing, during the life of a current local plan, might expose the authority to compensation claims from unhappy landowners who feel that the 'social housing quota' has reduced the development value of their land.

Guidance on Planning Agreements and Covenants

The Social Housing Unit of the House Builders Federation has issued a Guidance Note which sets out the broad principles which it believes should be taken into account when drawing up Section 106 Planning Agreements for social housing schemes in rural areas. These principles are equally applicable to schemes in urban areas.

■ The purpose of the scheme is to provide social housing. Sale housing will only be permitted to the extent that its existence can be demonstrated to be clearly necessary to subsidise the social housing.

■ Initial consumer costs should be specified for all social housing (including shared ownership). In preparing a social housing scheme developers should base their proposals on the income profile of those households identified by a village housing needs survey as requiring social housing and should demonstrate that social housing is being provided both initially and in the long term.

■ The long-term owner/manager of the properties should be party to the Section 106 Agreement. This organisation should be independent, non-profit distributing and subject to external security. It should therefore be either a housing association registered with the Housing Corporation or a Charitable Trust.

■ Priority will be given to people with a local connection who meet the housing association's normal criteria for letting or selling shared ownership housing to people in housing need.

The Association of District Councils (ADC) has summarised the contribution of restrictive covenants to this process:

"The Section 52 (now Section 106) Agreement will include covenants binding the initial signatories and their successors in perpetuity; this may require a clause allowing the signatories to nominate a successor in title, subject to the agreement of the others. The covenants will need to cover issues such as the number of units to be provided and on what tenure basis; target consumer costs for the rent and shared ownership housing; details of the priority groups who will have first access to the social housing; the definition of 'local'; the method by which the social housing will be allocated, and any information on nomination rights offered to the local authority and to any other agency (eg the landowner); and, where sale housing is involved, the phasing of the sale and social housing, and any rules about the first option going to people on the housing waiting list, and only then to other local people."

Example

Planning policies which seek to stimulate low cost social housing
Hereford And Worcester Structure Plan

This amended plan, and the policies it contains, has been approved by the Secretary of State for the Environment.

The plan states that:

"Within the general housing provision, planning authorities will seek to encourage proposals for the development of dwellings of types such as starter homes or low cost home ownership schemes, suitable for people not easily able to compete in the housing market. These proposals may call for relatively high densities on particular sites, and should be carefully designed to ensure that they are in keeping with their surroundings."

"Exceptionally, planning permission may be granted for low cost housing on land that would not normally be released for development, provided that:

■ The scheme would meet a genuine local need that would not otherwise be met

■ There are arrangements to ensure that the benefits of low cost housing will be enjoyed by subsequent occupants as well as the initial occupiers

■ Any such land released will be additional to the provision made for general housing demand in structure and local plans, and

■ The scheme otherwise satisfies the requirements for development in rural areas set out (elsewhere in the Structure Plan)

Within the green belt, small scale schemes may be permitted where suitable sites are available within existing settlements, but only those in those more extensive areas of green belt away from the urban fringe."

This policy is significant because despite specific mention of rural circumstances, it does not limit 'exceptional planning policy' initiatives to rural areas.

Further, the Secretary of State has been more flexible over green belt considerations than hitherto.

Example

Planning policies which seek to stimulate low cost social housing
West Sussex Structure Plan

This structure plan has also been approved by the Secretary of State for the Environment.

The plan states that:

"..there may occasionally be a case for limited additional release of land specifically to meet demand from people whose incomes are inadequate for normal house purchase, where there are few existing opportunities for meeting this demand in the vicinity."

"Some limited provision, additional to that in policy, may be made for the development of dwellings of types (such as starter homes or low cost home ownership schemes) suitable for people not easily able to compete in the existing housing market."

"This policy is intended to provide some scope to allow and encourage initiatives in solving the problem of housing lower income households in an area of high house prices. It will be used only in exceptional circumstances to take advantage of opportunities, and only where there is minimal conflict with environmental policies. It will allow the release of land outside the built up area (release inside the built up area being acceptable anyway). This policy does not imply development approval for any particular tenure. However, the initiatives will involve the participation of a District Council, housing association or other organisation with similar objectives for housing, able to engineer a package offering a substantial element of subsidy to the initial purchaser or tenant and, preferably, his successors."

"The provision of housing for rent or sale at prices which make it accessible to less affluent local people is as important in villages as elsewhere. (Development) should be small scale, and should be limited to villages with shops and services adequate to supply most basic convenience requirements, a primary school, some local employment, and public transport providing the opportunity to travel to work in a neighbouring town."

"In a few of the larger villages where there is a reasonable range of services the release of land for house building (for people who cannot afford home ownership) may be appropriate."

Example

Local Authorities and Housing Associations working together to make use of planning powers
The Cumbria Rural Housing Trust and the Cumbria County Land Bank Trust

The Cumbria Rural Housing Group (CHRG) is an enabling body which exists to promote and facilitate the development of new rural housing schemes. It does this by encouraging the positive involvement of local communities, local authorities, housing associations and other bodies.

CRHG is composed of representatives of Allerdale District Council, Eden District Council, South Lakeland District Council, Carlisle City Council, Copeland Borough Council, Cumbria County Council, the Northern Consortium of Housing Authorities, Northern Rock Housing Trust, Two Castles Housing Association, North Housing Association, Anchor Housing Association, the Housing Corporation, the Department of the Environment, the Rural Development Commission, the Country Landowners Association, the Lake District National Park Authority, Lancaster University, the Royal Institute of British Architects, the Royal Town Planning Institute, the House Builders Federation, Business in The Community and Voluntary Action Cumbria.

In practice, the local authorities and housing associations take the lead role.

The Cumbria Rural Housing Group can offer assistance to these organisations in the following areas:

■ With the identification of housing need by means of parish housing surveys carried out in partnership with the local community and Voluntary Action Cumbria.

■ By investigating methods of meeting this housing need - primarily through research into initiatives in other areas and an assessment of their applicability in Cumbria.

■ With the implementation of the identified solution - primarily by approaching and negotiating with funders, landowners, developers and local authority housing and planning officers.

During each stage the role of the Cumbria Rural Housing Group is to offer advice and/or practical assistance for the local community. The CRHG comprises people with a variety of skills such as dealing with rural housing problems, designing schemes to meet unusual needs, understanding planning constraints and obtaining development finance.

The CRHG has secured Housing Corporation approval for a total of seven housing projects in 1991-2, which will be developed by the associations represented on the Group in the areas of the local authorities represented on the Group.

In 1990, the CRHG established a Cumbria County Land Bank Trust which hopes to encourage both public and private sector landowners to dispose of land at low cost to support lower price rural housing. Its trustees include two members of the CRHG and a major local landowner.

Local landowners are being asked to offer suitable sites to the Land Bank Trust. In practice this will mean that the Land Bank Trust obtains an 'option' on the land for a period of five years. In return, the landowner will benefit from assistance in obtaining 'exceptional planning permission', by obtaining a higher price for their land as a consequence and by having the development 'legwork' undertaken by the Trust.

Ownership of the land will remain with the landowner until such time as a developer is identified who is prepared to develop the site in accordance with the objectives of the Trust. In the majority of cases the developer is likely to be a local housing association or village trust.

The Land Bank Trust will carry out such preliminary investigations regarding site servicing, planning permission, need and support for development, liaison with Parish Councils and local authorities and negotiations with private developers. The Trust will be responsible for ensuring that agreements are in place which secure that any low cost homes provided will be available to successive generations of local people.

The 'option' will then be exercised and the land will be transferred to the developer. The Trust will, where necessary, monitor the developer's activities to ensure that it is adhering to the agreement.

It is anticipated that most of the sites which are developed will be made available through 'exceptional planning permission'. This is indeed the case with the first two sites on which options are being negotiated.

CRHG employs one full time member of staff to undertake its work and to carry out administration and project management on behalf of the Land Bank Trust. The worker is based in the offices of Eden District Council and her wages are paid by the local authorities represented on the CRHG together with the National Park Authority and the Rural Development Commission.

Examples

Social Housing Schemes developed with the support of Local Planning Authorities

RURAL AREA
English Villages Housing Association
Welford-on-Avon, within the boundaries of Stratford-on-Avon
District Council

This village falls within the boundaries of Stratford-on-Avon District Council and the scheme was the first to take advantage of the 'exceptional planning permission for social housing' policy which was inserted into the District Council's local plan in 1989.

The site developed by the English Villages Housing Association (EVHA) was actually owned by Gloucester County Council and was allocated for agricultural use. In practice, it was only being used to provide grazing ground for sheep.

In association with the local parish council and EVHA, the Rural Housing Trust conducted a housing needs survey in the village. Public meetings were held to elicit the views of local residents. It was agreed that as the District Council was building 20 bungalows in the village, for elderly people to rent, the EVHA should concentrate on building low cost shared ownership homes. Westbury Partnership Homes won the tender to act as developer/contractor.

The landowner (Gloucester County Council), EVHA, the parish council and Stratford-on-Avon DC were co-signatories to a Section 52 (now Section 106) agreement that the development would be retained for social housing in perpetuity. The District Council granted exceptional planning permission and EVHA was therefore able to buy the site for less than a tenth of the value of land allocated for general needs housing in the area.

The shared ownership homes have been sold on a fixed equity arrangement. Purchasers are required to buy an initial equity share which covers all development and land costs. Two bedroom homes are being sold at £36,250 and three bedroom homes at £39,500. In most cases this represents about 50% of the current resale value of the property and requires a minimum household income of around £13,000 per annum.

Social Housing Schemes developed with the support of Local Planning Authorities

RURAL AREA
Warwickshire Rural Housing Association
Stretton-on-Fosse, within the boundaries of Stratford-On-Avon
District Council

The site for this development was owned by a local parish councillor who had previously tried, unsuccessfully, to provide low cost housing on the site. In this case, the parish council carried out a local housing need survey with the assistance of the Rural Housing Trust.

The survey demonstrated the extent of local housing need to Stratford-on-Avon District Council who responded by granting 'exceptional planning permission' for low cost housing development. The parish councillor then sold the site for £2,000 per building plot.

Warwickshire Rural Housing Association (WRHA) registered with the Housing Corporation in December 1989, bid for sufficient HAG for a scheme involving 10 houses for rent and received an actual allocation which enabled it to construct 7 rented homes. WRHA agreed that the English Villages Housing Association (EVHA) should develop 3 houses for sale on the rest of the site. EVHA were able to sell these houses for £39,250 compared to an estimated full market value of £70,000. WRHA started the construction of the homes for rent in November 1990 and anticipate that the likely rent will be £40-45 per week for two bedroom homes.

The site is governed by a Section 106 agreement limiting development to low cost housing for local people with priority being given (as in the Welford scheme noted above) to people living, working or having relatives within the village or to people who have had to move away from the village due to the lack of affordable accommodation but who now wish to return. The planning agreement also allows for those living in adjoining parishes to be considered in the event of lack of demand in the present or future. Stratford-on-Avon District Council is allowed to nominate people to occupy the property, provided that they meet the residence criteria.

Social Housing Schemes developed with the support of Local Planning Authorities

URBAN AREA
New Islington And Hackney Housing Association
Cornwallis Square, London Borough Of Islington

In a joint initiative, a consortium of associations (led by New Islington and Hackney Housing Association (NIHHA) and including Circle 33 Housing Trust and St George's Housing Trust) and Countryside Properties PLC developed 188 new homes on a site of 7 acres.

The site was owned by British Telecom and a local industrial concern and was used for a light engineering depot, workshops and warehousing. It had however become redundant to this former use and the owners sought to sell it for the best price. The owners hoped that the site would attract planning permission for housing development as it would thus become worth much more than if its existing industrial use was maintained.

London Borough of Islington was keen to stimulate the provision of social housing for local people on the site. The local authority's planning brief also made clear that any development should include provision of 1.5 acres of open space - to be secured by a Section 52 (now Section 106) agreement.

NIHHA and Countryside then persuaded the owners that although they could not offer as high a price as other developers they were likely to encounter much less opposition from London Borough of Islington, because of the inclusion in their scheme of a significant element of housing for rent. They would therefore be able to purchase the site much more quickly than other developers - who might take far longer to secure planning permission. On this basis the owners agreed to sell the site to the consortium and Countryside, who purchased it jointly.

Planning agreements were entered into between the London Borough of Islington, the consortium and Countryside under which the development partners agreed to transfer a part of the site to the London Borough of Islington for use as a car park and that NIHHA would have first option to acquire any property built by Countryside before it was sold on the open market.

The site was acquired in late 1987 and construction commenced in 1988. The development was completed in February 1991.

NIHHA and Circle 33 provided 65 homes for rent under a design and build contract with Countryside Properties, funded by the Housing Corporation. A further 18 homes were developed for shared ownership by St George's Housing Trust, also with Housing Corporation funding. Originally, it was proposed that the remaining 107 homes would be sold on the open market for outright owner occupation by Countryside. However, due to the slump in the property market which began in late 1988, NIHHA were able to purchase a further 89 of these homes for a mix of rented housing and shared ownership. Funding was provided by the Housing Corporation for 12 shared ownership dwellings, from the Area Health Authority for 6 care-in-the-community units and from the London Boroughs of Islington and Camden (through privately financed leaseback initiatives) for 71 homes for rent. In the end, 19 homes were sold by Countryside for outright owner occupation.

Social Housing Schemes developed with the support of Local Planning Authorities

URBAN AREA
East London Housing Association
Queen Mary's Hospital, London Borough of Newham

In a joint initiative, East London Housing Association and Countryside Properties PLC obtained exceptional planning permission to develop 118 new homes on a redundant hospital site of 3.7 acres.

Due to its proximity to Stratford shopping centre, the site had been allocated for commercial use in the local plan. However, Newham District Health Authority had received very little interest in the site from developers.

In a separate initiative, East London Housing Association had linked up with London and Quadrant Housing Association, London Borough of Newham and Newham District Health Authority to form a consortium to develop special needs housing in the area. The consortium placed particular emphasis on care-in-the-community projects. (See chapter on 'Special Needs Housing' for further details).

The consortium approached the Health Authority about the purchase of several of its redundant sites. Independently, the Health Authority decided to make it a condition of sale that at least part of these sites must be developed for care-in-the-community schemes. The Health Authority decided that any development of the Queen Mary's site must provide eight homes for people with multiple handicaps. ELHA agreed to prioritise the site within its development programme, to use its HAG allocation to meet the Health Authority requirement, and to develop as much social housing as possible on the rest of the site.

London Borough of Newham planners agreed to re-write the planning brief for the site, re-allocating it from commercial to housing use. At the same time, Newham planners decided to make the provision of care-in-the-community housing a requirement of planning permission on all redundant Health Authority sites. The planners successfully steered the new brief for the Queen Mary's site through a public consultation process.

At this point, ELHA and Countryside Properties tendered to purchase the site. Countryside's main role was that of contractor, but they also agreed to market any homes which ELHA could not purchase from within its HAG allocation.

The Kendon Trust, a charity assisting elderly people in Newham, agreed to provide capital funding of £2.5 million for a 40 unit sheltered scheme on the site. It was agreed that ELHA would manage these properties and Kendon would own the freehold.

In addition to the 40 sheltered units and the 8 'multiple handicap' units, Boleyn and Forest Housing Association (ELHA's home ownership subsidiary) was able to develop 48 homes for sale on a shared ownership basis. Using HAG, ELHA was also able to develop 27 houses with gardens for rent. Average net rents for all units are under £40 per week. ELHA did not need to take up Countryside's offer to market any surplus housing.

The development has been carried out to very high standards of design and construction. By placing the 'multiple handicap' units in the centre of the site, the possibility of objections from adjacent occupiers was removed and it is not possible to identify the different types of tenure on visual inspection. The design brief provided for an integrated scheme by specifying that general needs housing should be provided above the sheltered and special needs dwellings.

In the event, ELHA's offer of 100% nominations to the 'multiple handicap' units persuaded the Health Authority that they did not need to impose a restrictive covenant requiring a care-in-the-community scheme as a condition of sale. And the fact that ELHA and the Health Authority were part of the special needs consortium persuaded Newham Council planners that a formal planning agreement was not necessary.

5

URBAN RENEWAL

The purpose of this chapter is to explain how local authorities and housing associations can work together to achieve urban renewal.
The chapter covers:

■ the current legislative framework for urban renewal

■ the difficulties faced by authorities and associations seeking to undertake urban renewal activity

■ practical initiatives which can still be undertaken despite these difficulties

The Context

Urban renewal is the physical upgrading of run down urban or inner city areas.

The housing aspect of urban renewal involves the repair and modernisation of substandard dwellings, environmental works within renewal areas, new building on vacant infill sites and the replacement of derelict buildings. Repairs to existing buildings either take the form of external 'enveloping' works to whole streets of properties or of work to both the external and internal fabric of individual properties. Most of the properties in need of repair belong to low income owner occupiers or are part of the private rented sector.

Urban renewal is normally conducted on an area basis by local authorities and housing associations, centred around offices located in the heart of the renewal area, with participation by the local community.

Overall responsibility for urban renewal rests with local authorities. The new Section 605 of the Housing Act 1985 requires local authorities to:

■ consider the housing conditions in their district at least once a year in order to determine how best to use their powers to make grants for the purposes of improvement work,

■ to declare Renewal Areas (where appropriate)

■ to enforce regulations governing houses in multiple occupation, and

■ to initiate clearance activity

In the past, housing associations have been 'zoned' by local authorities (with the agreement of the Housing Corporation) to work in specific areas, often related to urban renewal programmes. Within these areas, associations would buy and rehabilitate unfit property. Decisions to purchase property were often taken on the basis of recommendations (known as 'referrals') made by the local authority. Housing associations have also collaborated with local authorities in environmental schemes and other measures to improve run down areas.

Urban renewal following The Local Government and Housing Act 1989

The 1989 Act overhauled the system of local authority funding and support for urban renewal. The new system came into effect in April and July 1990.

The main elements of the new system are:

■ a range of no less than 10 types of grant aid in all, some discretionary and some mandatory, known generically as 'renovation grants'. The term 'mandatory' means that the local authority must pay the grant and the term 'discretionary' means that it can choose whether to do so or not

■ all grants attract 75% government subsidy in the form of Specific Capital Grant.

■ a more rigorous method by which local authorities must decide whether renovation or demolition of unfit property is the 'most satisfactory course of action', before awarding renovation grants

■ Renewal Areas replace Housing Action Areas and General Improvement Areas as the focus of urban renewal activity - the new concept is very similar but the process of declaring a Renewal Area is far more complex than that of declaring Housing Action Areas and General Improvement Areas

■ Group Repair replaces Enveloping - the mechanism of tackling the outsides of complete terraces is retained but property owners now have to make means tested contributions instead of having the work done for free

Difficulties Facing Local Authorities And Housing Associations Wishing To Engage In Urban Renewal Activity

There has been a major reduction in urban renewal activity in the second half of the 1980's and in the early 1990's.

Local authority renovations in declared areas have fallen from 4,200 in 1982 to 2,800 today. The clearance of unfit property has also slumped from 40,000 demolitions in 1977 to 5,000 today.

Housing associations renovated 6,500 homes in Housing Action Areas and General Improvement Areas in 1982 but are now improving less than 1000 a year in urban renewal areas. Associations have reduced their bids for inner city rehab work and Housing Corporation resources are being redirected away from this activity. Rehab comprised 66% of the Corporation's Approved Development Programme in 1988-9 but accounted for less than 25% in 1989-90.

This reduction in urban renewal activity has occurred for two main reasons.

First, local authorities have lacked the capital finance to intervene directly or to make discretionary grants available.

The number of local authority grants awarded has fallen from a peak of 300,000 in 1983/4 to less than half this level now. Local authority funding of major repairs to those housing association properties which were originally rehabilitated using 'Local Authority HAG' has also fallen dramatically.

Second, housing associations have found it difficult to undertake urban renewal work under the 'mixed funding' regime.

Rehab work is often more expensive than new build and does not sit well with the current Housing Corporation emphasis on 'value for money'. New build on small sites is affected by the 'mixed funding' regime in much the same way. Rehab work is also more risky than new build, as structural problems which emerge during building work can produce punitive cost overruns from which associations are no longer fully indemnified by increased HAG payments.

Other difficulties, related to the Local Government and Housing Act 1989, compound this picture.

The means testing of renovation grants is likely to reduce demand from the most needy members of the community. Experience shows that all means tested benefits suffer from take-up problems. There must also be doubt whether sufficient private sector loan finance is available, in every case, to cover the proportion of costs which is not grant aided.

The replacement of enveloping with group repair schemes may also diminish the scope for urban renewal. Previously, works were undertaken free of charge but now property owners may have to pay up to 50% of costs (up to 25% if the property is situated in a Renewal Area) depending on their circumstances. This, in itself is likely to reduce take-up of grant. Housing associations do not qualify for local authority grant aid for group repair work to their properties.

The intensification of financial restrictions upon local authorities following the 1989 Act has made it even less likely that authorities will be able to make discretionary grants available or undertake the compulsory purchase of unfit property.

Nevertheless, there are some positive aspects to the new local authority grant regime. The abolition of limitations on the type of property that is eligible for grant, the removal of statutory limits on the cost of works, and the possibility of 100% grant aid for some applicants, may all provide a positive impetus to urban renewal.

Options for working together

Notwithstanding these difficulties, there is still some scope for local authorities and housing associations to undertake joint urban renewal activity.

The options can be briefly described as follows:

- direct local authority renovation grant funding for housing associations

- provision of 'Local Authority HAG' funding to housing associations for urban renewal activity

- sale by local authority of compulsorily purchased property, or other properties which need improvement, to housing associations

- housing associations acting as local authority agents by providing urban renewal services

- local authority support for housing association schemes bringing empty flats above shops into use with HAG funding

In practice, these options would work as follows.

Grants Available To Housing Associations

Housing associations are entitled to various urban renewal grants from their local authority on a means tested basis. These grants may provide a mechanism by which associations can undertake major repairs to properties which were originally built or rehabilitated using local authority capital funding.

The particular grants for which associations are eligible are as follows.

■ Mandatory Renovation Grants are designed to bring dwellings up to the newly defined standard of fitness. Renovation grants are mandatory if the local authority has served a Repair Notice on the property. The level of grant aid is fixed by a means test.

■ Common Parts Grants are available to help with the improvement or repair of the common parts of buildings containing one or more flats. This includes, for example, purpose-built mansion blocks and small scale conversions. Common Parts Grants will normally be discretionary, but will be mandatory if the local authority serves a repair notice on the housing association requiring works to be carried on the common parts of a particular property. The level of grant will be fixed by a means test.

■ Disabled Facilities Grants are available to make the home of a disabled person more suitable for them to live in, and to help the person manage more independently in the home. Again, the level of grant will be fixed by a means test.

The means test for housing associations (and private landlords) is based on the expected increase in rent, assessed by the Rent Officer, that will result from improvements. The size of a 10 year loan that could be repaid from this increase is calculated. Grant entitlement is then assessed as the difference between the cost of works and theoretical loan entitlement. If the work is judged unlikely to lead to a rent increase, any likely increase in capital value is taken into account.

Sale And Replacement Of Compulsorily Purchased Property By Local Authorities

The Local Authority (Capital Finance) Regulations 1990 provide an incentive for local authorities to sell compulsorily purchased property in order to obtain a capital receipt which can be employed to provide local authority rented accommodation. Housing associations are, naturally, potential purchasers of the compulsorily purchased housing.

Regulation 18 provides this incentive by allowing the authority to deduct expenditure related to these activities from the capital receipt obtained from the property sale leaving a smaller residual receipt from which 75% has to be set aside for debt redemption. (See chapter on 'Sale Of Local Authority Land' for a more detailed discussion of both debt redemption and the implications of 'deducted expenditure'.)

Regulation 18 stipulates that this incentive applies where 'the disposal is made pursuant to a compulsory purchase order and the land has been held by the local authority for the purposes of Part 2 of the Housing Act 1985 for a period of 2 years or more ending at the time of the disposal', and the property is sold in order to purchase another similar asset or to pay for works to a retained building or piece of land which is used for the provision of housing.

Where the capital receipt is obtained in the form of money, the local authority can offset the total cost of the following expenditure:

- the cost of newly acquired land
- works to any dwelling on that newly acquired land or on land already owned by the authority
- the cost of replacing that dwelling on existing or newly acquired land

provided that:

- the costs of the land and/or rebuilding or conversion are broadly equal to the reasonable cost of an equivalent replacement of the former building
- the decision to dispose of the land is made not more than 3 years before the disposal or receiving of receipts

The whole of the consideration received from the disposal can take 'the form of replacement land or the construction of or works to a building'. Where capital receipts take the form of non-monetary consideration the deduction is determined by reference to the value of land and/or buildings received.

Sale Of Acquired Dwellings Which Require Improvement

Local Authority (Capital Finance) Regulation 16 is ostensibly intended to stimulate 'acquisition for sale' initiatives, but can also be used to facilitate urban renewal.

The Regulation allows the original cost of the property, and of any subsequent works which were undertaken in order to facilitate its resale, to be deducted from the capital receipt obtained from the sale before debt redemption requirements are being calculated. (See chapters on the 'Sale Of Local Authority Land' and 'Stock Transfer' for further details of debt redemption and 'deducted expenditure').

However, property sold under Regulation 16 does not have to have been specifically acquired for resale - the decision to sell can come later. The only proviso is that the property must not have been let on a secure tenancy.

Therefore properties which have been kept empty, used for non-housing purposes or used for non-secure lettings (such as hostels or temporary accommodation) are covered by Regulation 16. No time limits apply.

For an illustration of how Regulation can be specifically employed see the example of Leicester City Council working with Foundation Housing Association which is given below.

Combining 'Local Authority HAG' And Mandatory Renovation Grants To Assist Housing Association In Urban Renewal Activity

Leicester City Council has developed a method of combining these sources of funding to enable housing associations to buy and repair unfit vacant properties which have been acquired by the local authority (for example as a result of a compulsory purchase order). The method works as follows.

A housing association purchases an empty local authority property using 'Local Authority HAG' funding. The capital receipt obtained from the housing association can be used, under the terms of Local Authority (Capital Finance) Regulation 16, to pay off the original purchase price of the property.

Once sold, the property is inspected by the local authority's Environmental Health

LA HAG, Renovation Grants and Regulation 16: Leicester City Council Model

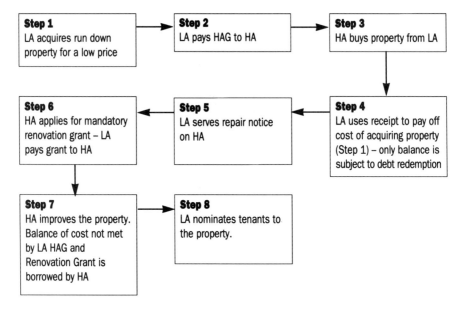

Step 1
LA acquires run down property for a low price

Step 2
LA pays HAG to HA

Step 3
HA buys property from LA

Step 6
HA applies for mandatory renovation grant – LA pays grant to HA

Step 5
LA serves repair notice on HA

Step 4
LA uses receipt to pay off cost of acquiring property (Step 1) – only balance is subject to debt redemption

Step 7
HA improves the property. Balance of cost not met by LA HAG and Renovation Grant is borrowed by HA

Step 8
LA nominates tenants to the property.

Officers and a statutory notice is served. This notice can either be a notice of unfitness or a Repair Notice requiring the property to be brought up to a reasonable standard of repair.

The service of these notices will give the association access to mandatory improvement grants which pay for a large part of the cost of repair works (subject to the means test).

The balance of the costs - that is costs not covered by HAG or the renovation grant - is funded on the basis of a privately financed loan taken out by the association.

In return for the provision of HAG, the local authority obtains nomination rights to the improved property. As 'Local Authority HAG' payments are reimbursed by the Housing Corporation, the only real cost to the authority relates to the payment of the mandatory renovation grant. These grants attract 75% government subsidy so the authority only has to find 25% of the grant sum.

Housing Association Led Agency Services

The government has recently announced that it is prepared to pay 50% of the running costs of agency services related to urban renewal - subject to annual decisions by the DoE on the overall amount of funding available. These agency services can be run by local authorities, housing associations or the private sector.

The purpose of agency services is to:

■ publicise grant availability

- deal with specific enquiries and means tests (both of which may require home visits)
- determine grant eligibility
- give advice on sources of borrowing
- agree specifications of works
- compare builders estimates, and
- pay out grants.

The agency may charge fees for this work and can undertake building work directly for a client. Given the complexity of the grant system and the need to provide an intensive 'client based' service there is clearly a significant role for specialist agencies in future urban renewal work.

The benefits to a local authority of employing housing associations - rather than private sector companies - as agents are:

- Housing associations are non profit making.

- Housing associations have substantial experience of renewal work and may have local offices and existing community links which can be used in an urban renewal initiative.

- Housing associations may have in-house resources - such as architects departments and direct labour organisations. DoE funded research by Bristol's School of Advanced Urban Studies has indicated that clients of private sector improvement agencies have suffered technical problems due to the separation of firms providing architectural or surveying services.

The benefits to a local authority of employing housing associations as agents - rather than setting up 'in house' agency services - are:

- Housing associations may be capable of operating more flexibly and may be able to provide a more responsive service to clients.

- Housing associations may already have local offices - thus saving the local authority the cost of setting these up.

- Using housing associations enables local authorities to experiment with agency services without setting them up as a permanent part of their own staffing establishment.

Indeed, in Scotland and Northern Ireland the use of housing associations as the lead agents in urban renewal is commonplace.

'Living Over The Shop' Schemes

In recent years, there has been a good deal of interest in bringing empty private and public sector homes back into use. This has led to some important practical innovations. These have included the steady increase in the use of 'short life' property for single homeless people, private sector leasing as a source of temporary accommodation for statutorily homeless households and the opening of the Land Registry to public inspection in 1990 (which makes the owners of empty homes more easily detectable).

One of the most significant innovations in this area has been the development of

Living Over The Shop schemes, which seek to bring unused residential accommodation over shops back into use or to turn unused storage space into accommodation. Much of the innovatory fieldwork in this area has been stimulated by the Rowntree and DoE funded 'Living Over The Shop' project which offers an advice service to property owners, local authorities and housing associations.

An important watershed in the development of Living Over The Shop initiatives was the Housing Act 1988 which, for the first time, permitted housing associations to acquire freehold or leasehold interests in part-commercial property and to finance such acquisitions through the use of HAG funding and under the terms of a business lease. The same Act also introduced assured shorthold tenancies which, although justifiably unpopular with private sector tenants, have at least (when employed within the terms of the business lease) enabled associations to offer an assurances to shop owners that they will be able to recover possession of flats above their shops should they wish to sell up and move on.

These Housing Act 1988 developments have meant that associations can now provide practical assistance to those local authorities seeking to bring empty buildings into use in order to ameliorate urban blight.

Research into the causes of vacancy, by the DoE and the Living Over The Shop project, have identified a variety of factors. These include greater wealth by shopkeepers which enables them to live in houses away from shop premises, more efficient transport systems which have contributed to the depopulation of town and city centres, increase in chain store domination of high streets, and the impact of computerised stock control which has reduced the need for storage. However, the research has also indicated that the fears of shop owners about the difficulty of obtaining possession have had a greater impact on the under-use of space above shops than any of the structural problems associated with bringing the accommodation up to an acceptable standard. The research indicates that initiatives will stand a greater chance of attracting interest if a comprehensive package covering funding, management and tenure options is presented to shop owners, as part of a co-ordinated approach by authorities and associations. The association or one council department should act as a 'lead partner' in terms of dealing with shop owner queries.

Living Over The Shop schemes can have the following benefits:

Property Owners

■ Increased security for the commercial premises underneath the flat

■ Improvements enhance the capital value of the entire building

■ Owner receives rental income (net of the housing association's management, maintenance and loan repayment costs)

■ The fabric of the property is maintained

Local Authorities

■ Prevents city or town centres from 'dying' and reduces crime and vandalism in the vicinity

■ In doing so, increases income for adjacent businesses

■ Increases the stock of small rented units of accommodation in the area

■ Historic buildings can be preserved in this way

■ Local authority owned flats over shops are eligible for HAG funding (see below)

Housing Associations

■ Provides good quality temporary accommodation - 'temporary' can mean 5 to 20 years depending on the terms of the lease

■ As the accommodation is centrally located it is ideal for mobile elderly people - although it is far less suitable for homeless households with young children

The Housing Corporation has indicated a keen interest in providing capital funding for Living Over The Shop Schemes. Its approach has been to make HAG available on a 'pilot' basis and to determine fixed schemework procedures after observing scheme development. In the meantime, each scheme is being judged on its merits, with the level of HAG being determined according to scheme feasibility and value for money (which are both partly determined by the length of any lease obtained). HAG is available on local authority owned flats over shops where a leasehold interest is granted to a housing association. The Corporation has made allocations of HAG available to associations in seven of its nine regions in 1991-2.

The other potential source of funding for Living Over The Shop schemes is renovation grants. However, the means test is likely to act as a disincentive because the greater the increase in potential rental income or capital value the less grant will be available for works. This problem might be overcome by using HAG to 'top up' renovation grants. However, at the time of writing, the Housing Corporation has yet to take a view on this approach.

Example

Use of Regulation 16 in the context of Urban Renewal
Leicester City Council And Foundation Housing Association

In 1991, Leicester City Council disposed of a property in St Stephens Road, Leicester to Foundation Housing association under the terms of Regulation 16.

The property had been acquired by the City Council at some time in the past and had been used as a womens aid hostel until the womens aid group (who were managing the property) folded.

The City Council was keen to support the work of Foundation Housing Association which specialises in housing for Afro-Caribbean people. As the property was located in an area the association worked in, both parties were interested in a property transfer. The proposal worked well from the City Council's point of view because, having been in use as a hostel with rooms having been let on the basis of licenses rather than secure tenancies, the original acquisition cost may be deducted from the receipt obtained from Foundation Housing Association.

The property is now in use, providing accommodation for homeless Afro-Caribbean women.

Example

A living over the shop project

8 Ironmonger Street, Stamford, Lincolnshire

Minster General Housing Association and South Kesteven District Council

This four storey listed building, built in 1790, is being refurbished as rented accommodation at the time of writing. It is the first scheme to be funded through a combination of HAG and local authority funding. The project will convert the three floors above a charity shop into three self contained units.

The property was identified by the 'Living Over The Shop' project, which contacted Minster General Housing Association to suggest that it be brought into use. The association then secured a 20 year business lease on the property under the terms of the Landlord And Tenant Act 1954 Part 2 which guarantees owners vacant possession on a fixed date. No premium was required and the net rent, currently around £3,000 per year, will be reviewed every five years in line with the Retail Price Index. Lettings will be made on the basis of assured shorthold tenancies.

Refurbishment costs of £66,000 are being met by HAG at 70%, a 25% contribution from the property owner and with 5% provided by the local authority through Town Scheme grant. South Kesteven District Council will obtain 100% nomination rights to the flats.

South Kesteven District Council has agreed to allocate £50,000 towards Living Over The Shop schemes in 1991-2 which it hopes to combine with future HAG funding.

6

SPECIAL NEEDS HOUSING

This chapter will outline:

■ the context in which special needs schemes are developed

■ the sources of funding available

■ the potential for local authorities to play a strategic role

■ the range of opportunities for authorities and associations to work together

■ the particular contribution that can be made by special needs housing consortia

It is not proposed to replicate the authoritative good practice literature which has been produced by the National Federation Of Housing Associations. The attention of readers is drawn, in particular, to the following NFHA publications -'Housing: The Foundation Of Community Care' (NFHA 1989) and 'Housing Consortia For Community Care' (NFHA 1988).

Instead, the text will concentrate upon financial and practical aspects of local authority and housing association partnerships in respect of special needs housing.

The Context

Client Groups With Special Needs
Central to any definition of special needs housing is the provision of care and support in addition to accommodation.

Many special needs schemes are developed by housing associations but are managed on their behalf by specialist agencies. A smaller proportion of special needs schemes are directly managed by housing associations. Some housing associations, such as Stonham HA or Look Ahead HA, specialise in this form of housing.

The Housing Corporation classes the following groups as potential clients for special needs housing:

■ frail elderly people

■ people with physical disabilities

■ people with learning difficulties (still sometimes referred to as people with mental handicaps)

■ people with mental health problems

■ people with drug or alcohol related problems

■ people leaving penal establishments or on probation

■ refugees

■ women at risk of domestic violence

■ vulnerable women with children

■ young people at risk or leaving care

■ single homeless people

■ people with AIDS/ARC or who are HIV positive

People with special needs require varying types of assistance. In some cases, their existing homes will require physical adaptation; in others the main need is for intensive management and/or the provision of care.

It is generally accepted that people with special needs should have the opportunity to live and receive support in their own homes.

However, there will continue to be some people who will require rehousing into specialised accommodation. These will include people being discharged from institutions or residential care homes who do not have a home of their own, people whose family or relatives cannot cope with the caring role and people living in accommodation which exacerbates their problems.

For simplicity, special needs housing projects can be divided into low care and high care. Low care schemes assume a fair degree of independence on the part of the resident and offer support in terms of resettlement, welfare benefits advice and general befriending. High care schemes assume less resident independence and offer a higher element of care and support.

This support can range from:

■ help in developing basic life skills

■ personal care (cooking, cleaning, assistance with personal hygiene)

■ full medical support

Obviously, high care schemes have higher running costs than low care schemes. This is particularly so where high care schemes are provided on a small scale.

Care in the Community

Government policy advocates the closure of institutions caring for people with learning difficulties or mental illness and their replacement with 'care in the community' facilities. These are generally defined as smaller, more humane accommodation which may include small hostels, shared housing, cluster flats or individual dwellings with support services being provided to people in their home.

Homelessness and Special Needs

As we have noted, homeless people come within the Housing Corporation's definition of special needs if they are vulnerable or in need of care and/or support (including resettlement support). Homeless people without special needs are dealt with under the Corporation's general needs programme.

Under the 1981 'hostels initiative', special needs funding was the main government response to the needs of single homeless people. In recent years, however, the Corporation has sought to provide permanent accommodation rather than hostels.

Currently, there are two government-funded initiatives related specifically to people who are sleeping rough in London.

The first, known as the 'rough sleepers initiative', primarily involves the dispensation of funds by the Housing Corporation. Announced in June 1990, it made £15 million available during 1990/1 for housing associations to provide accommodation and services for people living on the streets. Although most of the units created have been in direct access hostels and property temporarily leased from the private sector, around 400 permanent units have been provided. In 1991-3, a further £81 million is being made available for housing associations (in partnership with specialist management organisations) mainly to provide longer term accommodation for the same client group. Again, the funding will be primarily administered by the Housing Corporation.

Second, the 'homeless and mentally ill' initiative, announced in July 1990 and funded by the Department of Health makes £5 million available to provide accommodation and psychiatric care for mentally ill people sleeping rough on the streets of London. The programme will include the funding of additional specialist short term hostel places and new community-based outreach psychiatric teams. The initiative will not provide funds for the provision of longer term accommodation. (See example given below of Look Ahead Housing Association's Varden Street hostel for further details).

Funding Special Needs Schemes

As will become evident, the special needs housing field consists of a wide range of funding agencies.

The primary sources of capital and revenue funding are as follows.

CAPITAL FUNDING

Housing Corporation - Housing Association Grant (HAG)

HAG is the main source of capital funding for special needs projects developed by registered housing associations.

Unlike general needs projects, special needs schemes are eligible for 100% HAG funding with no requirement to raise private finance.

To qualify for 100% HAG, special needs schemes must satisfy certain eligibility criteria. The key criteria are:

■ the primary purpose of the scheme must be the provision of housing with the care element being a secondary factor

■ the scheme must provide an intensive level of housing management and services appropriate to the special needs of its client group - a minimum staff to resident ratio is being determined at the time of writing

■ the scheme must not provide 'time limited' emergency accommodation without resettlement support (eg nightshelters)

■ the scheme must not fulfil a function which is the statutory responsibility of another agency (eg bail hostels and the Home Office)

■ the scheme must not involve the transfer of tenanted local authority stock (such as local authority owned registered care homes).

Local Authority

Social service authorities - county councils in all except the metropolitan areas - have the power to provide capital funding to housing associations and other voluntary sector agencies which provide residential care to people for whom the authority has a statutory responsibility - such as young people in care and frail elderly people. They have no powers to fund 'ordinary' housing.

Housing departments can provide capital finance for any housing project subject to the sole limitation of government spending constraints. (See chapter on 'Financial Assistance For Housing Associations').

Health Authority Funding

District health authorities can fund special needs housing schemes from either their mainstream budget or their joint finance budget. The term 'mainstream budget' describes money from the Department of Health which is allocated via the regional health authorities. The term 'joint finance budget' describes a much smaller amount of money obtained directly from the Department of Health and allocated jointly by district health and local authorities in its area, at a forum known as the Joint Consultative Committee.

Projects related to hospital closures are funded under the joint finance mechanism. Priority is generally given to schemes housing people who are elderly, or suffering from mental illness or who have learning difficulties. Projects which are not related to hospital closures are funded directly by the health authority from its mainstream budget. The power of health authorities to provide capital funding for housing schemes is limited to support for registered housing associations.

Department of Health joint finance guidelines state that, normally, capital allocations should not exceed two thirds of the total cost, although the health authority has discretion to meet the total cost if it wishes. Unfortunately, voluntary sector bids for joint funding are in competition with bids from both the health authority and the local authority themselves.

Home Office Funding

The Home Office is empowered to provide funding for after care accommodation and hostels for ex-offenders or people who are 'at risk of offending'. Funding arrangements are based on area accommodation strategies developed by local discussion forums (which include probation service, local authority and voluntary sector representatives). These strategies are then approved by the area probation committee and forwarded to the Home Office for payment.

To be eligible for Home Office funding, projects must have a locally appointed management committee which includes a senior member of the area probation service. Organisations are not required to reserve Home Office funded places exclusively for people referred by the probation service - provided that the people housed fit within the Home Office criteria (see above).

Limited capital grants are available to projects (which receive revenue funding from the Housing Corporation) to help carry out improvements to meet fire precaution or public health regulations or to improve staff accommodation. Other small grants are occasionally made in respect of urgent, non-recurrent items such as vehicles or equipment.

Dept Of Social Security (DSS) Funding

The DSS has, in the past, provided funding for housing associations which have assisted in the replacement of DSS-run short stay accommodation (variously termed nightshelters or resettlement units) for homeless people "with an unsettled way of life". However, the closure of these units has been postponed and funding of new projects discontinued.

REVENUE FUNDING

Charges To Residents

Charges to residents are the primary source of revenue funding for special needs schemes. Residents normally pay these charges with the help of state benefits.

Housing costs are met from housing benefit, with payments limited to market rent.

Income support payments to residents (in theory) cover items such as food and other household expenditure.

Generally, the cost of care services is not eligible for housing benefit or Income Support subsidy, although specific benefits (such as Attendance Allowance) may be able to fund part of the care costs.

Residents of hostels which are registered under the Registered Homes Act 1984 still have housing and care costs met by the Department of Social Security. However, this method of payment is set to end in April 1993, when it is likely that housing benefit will pick up housing costs and local authority social service departments will become responsible for care costs.

Housing Corporation - Special Needs Management Allowance (SNMA)

This funding is paid by the Housing Corporation to cover the recurrent non-care costs of hostel or self contained housing projects managed by registered housing associations and meeting the HAG eligibility criteria identified on page 77. SNMA is payable for all new special needs schemes approved from April 1991. SNMA replaces Hostel Deficit Grant as the means by which the Corporation provides revenue funding for special needs schemes. All existing projects currently receiving Hostel Deficit Grant will switch to SNMA funding over a period of 5 years starting from April 1992. SNMA is paid on a flat rate per bedspace.

Schemes where capital costs have not been met by HAG, will not normally be eligible for SNMA.

However, exceptions may be made, at the discretion of the Housing Corporation (and dependent upon the availability of resources), for schemes where:

■ property has been leased by local authorities

■ where capital costs have been met by charitable funds, and

■ where former housing association general needs housing is now being used for special needs.

No exception can be made for schemes where capital costs have been funded by the Department of Health or the Home Office or the Department of Social Security.

Housing Corporation - Wardens Cost Element

It is possible for associations to claim an additional management allowance - the warden's cost element - if they are rehousing, within their ordinary housing stock, people who are 'moving on' from hostels, group homes, hospitals and other institutions and who require some additional support. However, the future of Wardens Cost Element is presently under review.

Top Up Funding

This is normally required to cover the cost of particular kinds of care or intensive management or the risk of higher voids/lost rent associated with particular types of special need project.

The source of top up funding is largely dependent upon the nature of the client group. Where the project has a specific client group with a limited range of needs, their appropriate funding source may be clear. For example, the Home Office might fund hostels for ex-offenders. Other projects may involve a mixed client group with a range of needs and no single funder may be prepared to take responsibility. In such cases, the managing agency will need to arrange a package of top up funding from various sources.

Local authorities can provide top up funding for special needs schemes. Local social services authorities are able to fund any voluntary body providing services of a kind which the authority itself could provide - such as services for people with a physical handicap or learning difficulties, people with mental health problems, people with an alcohol or drug abuse problem, or elderly people. Local authority housing committees have general powers to provide revenue funding to voluntary sector projects under Section 73 of the Housing Act 1985, Section 137 of the Local Government Act 1972 or by using Urban Programme funds.

Health authority funds can provide top up funding for special needs schemes run by any type of voluntary organisation (including specialist management agencies which are not registered with the Housing Corporation). Revenue payments can be made, for between three and thirteen years, under the joint finance system regardless of whether the project has received capital finance from the health authority. Payments from the mainstream allocation can only be used to support voluntary sector projects which enable people to leave hospital, but these payments can be made for an indefinite period. This type of payment is normally related to savings in hospital care made by the health authority and is often known as a 'dowry' payment.

Home Office supported projects normally receive revenue funding as follows. Where a project is receiving HDG/SNMA from the Housing Corporation, Home Office funding is available on a flat rate basis for 'excess management costs' related to the provision of care and support. In some cases, where the project does not receive SNMA, the Home Office may be prepared to make a flat rate grant towards a project's deficit.

Charitable funds, from a wide variety of organisations are a common source of top-up funding.

Local Authority strategic role

At a national level, there is little evidence of a co-ordinated funding strategy involving the Department of the Environment, the Department of Health, the Department of Social Security and the Home Office.

At a local level, the joint finance arrangements provide a degree of co-ordination between local authorities and district health authorities. However, housing associations and other voluntary agencies are often forced to compete unnecessarily for an indeterminate package of funds.

Clearly, the situation would be improved if one body took overall responsibility at a local level for developing and co-ordinating a special needs housing strategy.

This co-ordinating role would have three primary facets - needs assessment, planning and finance.

Local authorities are best placed to undertake this role.

Under the Housing Act 1985, local authority housing departments have responsibility for the assessment of local housing needs. Part of this brief should be the identification of special needs in the authority's area. This work should be undertaken in consultation with district health authorities, the local probation service, voluntary sector care agencies, housing associations working in the area and the regional office of the Housing Corporation.

Both county and district councils can use their planning powers to assist the development of special needs housing schemes, by including positive policies in both structure and local plans. Clear statements on the number of special needs or mobility housing units to be provided, as a proportion of general needs housing units, will help produce a positive response amongst developers and create development opportunities for housing associations. Planning briefs for particular sites could specify the need for a specific number of special needs units. (See example of Queen Mary's Hospital, London Borough of Newham in section on 'Use of Local Authority Planning Powers' for evidence of the feasibility of this approach.)

Local authorities could also liaise with other statutory funding agencies to identify capital and revenue resources which are available in its area and, in discussion with all interested parties, make recommendations for targeting those funds towards the special needs which have been identified.

Finally, local authorities can advise the Housing Corporation on local special needs priorities (as many already do) and target land sales towards specific schemes.

Example

West Suffolk Liaison Structure

The voluntary and statutory agencies in West Suffolk, in common with others throughout the country, are grappling with the twin difficulties of producing realistic plans for special needs initiatives and developing liaison structures which will lead to the implementation of their plans.

There is clearly no one right model to follow. The geography and demography of each area, together with the overlap of various authorities and agencies involved, will determine the precise structure introduced. However, the West Suffolk Liaison Structure demonstrates the complexity of the task and suggests how it might be tackled.

In West Suffolk, there is well established liaison between the West Suffolk Health Authority, Suffolk County Council social services department and the housing departments of the district councils which fall (completely or partly) within the health authority area - namely St Edmundsbury DC, Forest Heath DC, Mid Suffolk DC and Babergh DC. These organisations now meet together as the Joint Care Purchasing Team to determine the use of health authority 'joint finance'.

The Joint Care Purchasing Team (JCPT) is composed of over 20 officers from these

West Suffolk 'Special Needs' Liaison Structure

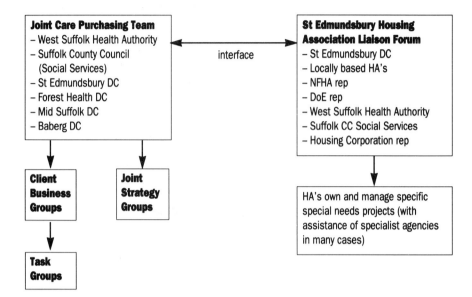

Joint Care Purchasing Team
– West Suffolk Health Authority
– Suffolk County Council (Social Services)
– St Edmundsbury DC
– Forest Health DC
– Mid Suffolk DC
– Baberg DC

interface

St Edmundsbury Housing Association Liaison Forum
– St Edmundsbury DC
– Locally based HA's
– NFHA rep
– DoE rep
– West Suffolk Health Authority
– Suffolk CC Social Services
– Housing Corporation rep

Client Business Groups

Joint Strategy Groups

HA's own and manage specific special needs projects (with assistance of specialist agencies in many cases)

Task Groups

organisations. In addition to the allocation of money, the team monitors the development of special needs housing in broad terms. To date most of the joint finance allocations to specific projects has been in the form of revenue, with capital funding coming primarily from the Housing Corporation. As the JCPT is an officer group, its decisions have to be ratified by the elected health and local authority members who meet as the Joint Finance Council.

To help it in its work, the JCPT has set up Client Business Groups (CBGs) to implement the overall plans. The CBGs decide upon individual projects and set up ad-hoc Task Groups to work on the detail of these projects. The Task Groups invite particular housing associations to join in the discussions when the proposed projects fall within those associations' areas of expertise or geographical areas of operation.

Another element of this complex structure are Joint Strategy Groups which advise the JCPT on future policy in relation to particular client groups.

At a regional level, therefore, the allocation of health authority finance, the origination of plans to use that finance, and the proposals for specific projects are dealt with in a co-ordinated manner.

The actual development of schemes takes place at district council level.

Within the Borough of St Edmundsbury, for example, the system works as follows. The Chief Housing Officer of St Edmundsbury DC convenes a Housing Association Liaison Forum which includes representatives from each of the associations working in the district plus representatives from the Housing Corporation, the Department of the Environment, the National Federation of Housing Associations, the West Suffolk Health

Authority and Suffolk County Council social services department.

The Housing Association Liaison Forum 'locks into' the broader Joint Care Planning Team decision making process by preparing a co-ordinated bid from local associations for Housing Corporation funding for the special needs projects prioritised by the JCPT. The final decision on this matter, of course, rests with the Corporation. St Edmundsbury DC assists in this process by articulating its own strategy for special needs housing.

Two things are evident from this example. First, the complexity of structures required to bring together all the health, local authority and housing association partners involved in developing community based special needs housing. Second, the key role of the local housing authority. St Edmundsbury DC takes part in the decisions about the allocation of joint finance at the Joint Care Planning Team, the implementation of overall plans at the Client Business Group, the origination of client group strategies at the Joint Strategy Group, the detail of specific projects at the Task Groups and the formulation of housing association bids to the Housing Corporation by convening the Housing Association Liaison Forum.

Range of special needs housing partnership possibilities

The range of partnership possibilities between local authorities and housing associations is unlimited, but includes:

- capital and revenue funding support
- land and property sales
- move-on accommodation
- leasing of property
- care support arrangements

The range is best demonstrated by the following example.

Example

South Yorkshire Housing Association (SYHA) and Sheffield City Council

South Yorkshire Housing Association and Sheffield City Council work together in the following ways.

Revenue 'Top Up' Funding

This money is primarily paid by the Family and Community Services Department - Sheffield City Council's term for social services - or from its Education Department. The precise source of funding may be mainstream grant aid budgets, Urban Programme finance or 'joint finance' with the Health Authority. Education powers are used to support schemes working with young people aged 16-18 which have a 'youth-work' element.

Move-on Housing

SYHA, and the agencies who manage most of its special needs schemes, rely heavy on Sheffield City Council for move-on accommodation - particularly for self contained single person units. The City Council provides a tenancy support service for ex-residents of special needs schemes who have been allocated council property. Local housing associations operate a separate but similar support service covering non-council stock.

Local Authority HAG

Several schemes were developed by SYHA in the early 1980's using capital finance provided by the City Council through the 'LA HAG' mechanism, including a hostel for young single people and a refuge for women who have suffered domestic violence.

Sale Of Council Buildings

Sheffield City Council has sold 'sundry' properties to SYHA at less than market value. One large detached house with a garden, for example, was developed by SYHA as a scheme for people with learning difficulties using Housing Corporation funding. Properties held by committees other than the housing committee, such as redundant children's homes, are particularly useful in this context. SYHA is interested in any such property, provided that there is sufficient prior notice of disposal to enable it to raise capital and revenue funding.

Leasing Of Property

SYHA has leased several properties from the City Council on a short-life basis and has made them habitable using Housing Corporation 'Mini-HAG' funding. Provided that these properties can be brought up to an acceptable standard of fitness using Mini-HAG, and are leased at a peppercorn rent, they are very useful for schemes where only short-term security of tenure is required. Readers are advised to consult 'Filling The Empties' (Shelter 1990) for further details of short-life housing and 'Mini-HAG' funding.

Sale Of Land

There are many examples of Sheffield City Council selling SYHA land for developments which include special needs housing. One recent example involved a site on which SYHA developed 40 units including two homes for people with learning difficulties.

Housing Committee Grant Aid

The Housing Committee has provided grants towards the admin costs of the Voluntary Housing Forum which co-ordinates housing association hostel and homelessness projects in the city. The Forum has a formal role representing the voluntary sector on the City Council's Hostels and Homeless Working Party and its Special Needs Working Party. The Housing Committee also provides grant aid to the Women's Housing Forum.

Support Agreements

Staff from the Council's Family and Community Services Department provide care and support to tenants with special needs who are resident in certain SYHA owned registered care homes - such as people with learning difficulties who are leaving long stay hospital, people with mental health problems and frail elderly people. This approach developed because the Council was having financial difficulties in developing its own care-in-the-community schemes. It had skilled and experienced staff who could help housing associations but it staff wished to retain these staff within the F&CS Department. The Council staff involved in these initiatives provide care services to SYHA on a contractual basis. SYHA supervises overall provision and undertakes all housing management functions. SYHA and the City Council are considering the formal secondment of these staff. The Health Authority provides 'top up' revenue support for many of these schemes.

Other Initiatives

SYHA and Sheffield City Council are currently discussing the feasibility of transferring council-owned elderly persons homes, hostels for people with learning difficulties and further 'short-life' properties.

Special Needs housing consortia

One specific form of partnership which is worth looking at in greater detail is the establishment of a special needs housing consortium.

The function of a special needs housing consortium is to carry out strategic planning, funding and care provision for people with special needs, in a co-ordinated manner. It has been estimated that there are more than 50 special needs housing consortia in England and Wales. Most have been set up in response to the planned closure of long stay hospitals as part of the government's 'care in the community' programme (see above). Most work within either a single health or local authority boundary.

The consortium is a voluntary agency with independent legal status, usually registered as an Industrial or Provident Society or as a registered charity or as a company limited by guarantee.

Its multi agency membership is likely to include health authorities, local authorities (social services and housing departments), housing associations and other voluntary organisations. Following Section 69 of the Local Government And Housing Act 1989, local authority membership of the consortium's management committee cannot equal or exceed 20% without the consortium being deemed to be an 'influenced company' and being subject to the local authority's financial regime and controls.

The main purpose of the consortium is usually the provision of housing, with the consortium commonly contracting with either the health or local authority regarding the provision of care support and staff.

Client groups usually include the people discharged from these long stay hospitals, notably people with learning difficulties, mental illness and frail elderly people. However, there is no actual limit to the range of groups served and some consortia are now, for example, taking over registered care homes previously owned and managed by local authority social services departments.

Among the objectives of special needs housing consortia are:

■ to speed up the discharge of residents from long stay hospitals managed by health and social services authorities into smaller scale accommodation, and thus enable these people to gain access to housing benefit and Income Support to help pay for the cost of their housing and care support - thus enabling the authorities to save money

■ to gain access to financial resources which would not be available to individual agencies operating interdependently of one another, through pooling the capital and revenue funds to which member agencies have access - thus housing associations get guaranteed access to local authority and health authority funding and those statutory agencies gain indirect access to HAG.

■ to make services available on a co-ordinated basis and to pool the skills, knowledge and experience of individual agencies in order to offer a better service.

■ to create a joint budget which is not controlled by a single agency.

■ to provide a more open decision making process in which housing associations and other voluntary agencies can have a greater influence

■ to enable member agencies to concentrate on what they are best equipped to do - with housing associations undertaking the housing management function and health and social service authorities undertaking the care function.

The operation of a special needs consortium is best demonstrated by reference to a specific example.

Example

Newham Special Needs Housing Consortium

The idea for a consortium originated from East London Housing Association (ELHA) which was working in the London Borough of Newham.

The stimulus was twofold.

First, there was concern about the implications of the impending closure of two local long-stay hospitals.

Second, there was the commitment of £850,000 capital funding by the Housing Corporation to ELHA and London & Quadrant Housing Trust to develop special needs housing.

This seemed to create the opportunity for the practical implementation of an integrated planning, housing and care strategy.

The consortium was constituted in July 1987 with the following objects:

"To relieve persons within the London Borough of Newham who are mentally handicapped, mentally ill and persons in other priority care groups by the provision of housing for such persons and by the provision of such other forms of assistance for the benefit of such persons as may be deemed desirable."

Newham Special Needs Housing Consortium

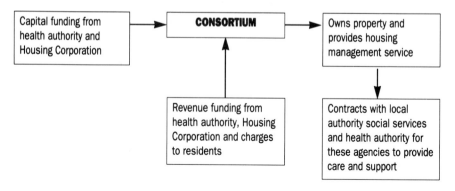

The Consortium adopted four specific functions:

■ to act as a forum for the co-ordination of capital and revenue finance

■ to act as a management agency for special needs housing for priority care groups

■ to act in advisory capacity to the local authority and health authority

■ to enter into contracts with the local authority and the health authority regarding the provision of care to residents living in property managed by the consortium

The following agencies are represented on the consortium:

■ Newham District Health Authority

■ London Borough of Newham

■ East London Housing Association

■ London & Quadrant Housing Trust

■ MIND

■ MENCAP

There is a two tier management structure. The consortium is managed by twelve directors - including politicians from the local authority, members of the health authority and one management committee person each from ELHA and L&Q, a former local authority member who is now an 'independent' director and a local accountant. In practice the directors are led, in their decision making, by recommendations from the management group composed of officers from the agencies which are represented in the consortium - such as the health and local authorities and the local MIND and MENCAP groups.

The consortium is staffed by a general manager, a housing officer (development), two housing officers (management), a further part-time housing officer (management), a part-time administrator, a part-time treasurer, a finance officer and a clerk/typist.

Capital funding has been provided by the Housing Corporation and the District Health Authority. Revenue funding has been provided by the District Health Authority, the Housing Corporation and from charges to residents. It is hoped that, eventually, the consortium staff will be paid from rents from properties in its management.

The local authority social services department and the District Health Authority have provided care and support (on the basis of a legal contract with the consortium) for people with learning difficulties living in houses managed by the consortium. The local authority housing department has played a strategic role, assessing sites for special needs use and dealing with the homelessness implications of the hospital closure.

The consortium currently manages 74 bedspaces in a range of homes with between 3 and 9 places each. Around one sixth of these places are for people with mental illness and the remainder are for people with learning difficulties. There are another 80 bedspaces under development. At present, all the homes are registered under the Registered Homes Act 1984.

Most of the accommodation developed by the consortium has been allocated to people leaving the South Ockenden (mental handicap) and Goodmayes (psychiatric) hospitals. Day-to-day running of the accommodation is carried out by the consortium's housing officers in liaison with the senior care manager in each house.

The consortium is considering the transfer of registered care homes owned and managed by the local authority. Although this type of initiative would represent a move away from the consortium's small scale non-institutional development and management ethos, it would engender much needed financial stability.

East London Housing Association is now involved, in a similar manner, in seven other special needs consortia.

Examples of specific projects

Homelesness and Mental Ill-Health
The Varden Street Project
Look Ahead Housing Association, LB Tower Hamlets Social Services Department, North East Thames Regional Health Authority and others.

This project arose out of a Department of Health initiative, which commenced in early 1990, to identify and help people with severe mental health problems who were sleeping rough in central London. The Department of Health guaranteed funding for three of London's four Regional Health Authorities, initially to allow each authority to develop a residential unit as first stage accommodation for these people. At the same time the Department of Health provided revenue funding for small outreach teams of workers who will make contact with, and help, mentally ill homeless people.

The North East Thames Regional Health Authority developed two separate responses to this initiative. The one involving the City and East London concerns us here. A steering group was set up involving representatives from the City of London Corporation, City and Hackney Health Authority, LB Tower Hamlets, local voluntary agencies working with homeless people and the East London Homeless Health Primary Care Team.

The East London Homeless Health Primary Care Team was chosen to co-ordinate the work of the outreach team. Its management committee includes representatives from LB Tower Hamlets, City and Hackney Health Authority and other interested agencies.

The steering group chose Look Ahead Housing Association to develop the residential initiative in their area. City and Hackney District Health Authority and the London Borough of Tower Hamlets social services department have representatives on the committee formed to manage the project.

The aims of the residential project are to:

■ provide temporary accommodation and a supportive environment to homeless people with mental health problems (primarily referred by the East London Homeless Health Primary Care Team outreach workers)

■ provide appropriate support for residents as part of a structured rehabilitation programme agreed with the residents

■ prepare and assist residents in obtaining access, and moving on, to permanent housing

■ ensure that residents obtain access to relevant mainstream health, social and other services in accordance with their needs

The residential accommodation is situated in the Whitechapel area and is an adaptation of a building, originally built as self contained flats, to provide 11 units of supported accommodation. Each resident has their own bedroom and, in most cases, their own bathroom and toilet. Kitchen facilities are shared between the two or three residents. Each flat and room will have a lockable door and the building has a main entrance door. The accommodation is fully furnished. In addition, there is a flat providing a communal dining room/kitchen, a communal lounge, laundry facilities and an office and a sleep-over room for staff.

One main meal a day will be provided in the communal dining room. Residents will be encouraged and assisted, where appropriate, to prepare other meals themselves. The project is to be registered under the Registered Homes Act 1984. There will be a team of 10 staff to manage the project. Staff will provide 24 hour cover, every day of the year, with a minimum of two staff on duty at any one time.

The capital cost of the project was £737,500. This included the building, adaptations, furniture and equipment, and associated legal, professional and development administration costs. This is being funded by a grant from the Department of Health, paid direct to Look Ahead Housing Association.

The revenue costs of the project are being funded by charges to residents (at the registered home rate) and by an additional grant from the Department of Health which is paid via London Borough of Tower Hamlets Social Services Department. For the year 1991-2, this has been agreed at a level of £14,000 per bedspace (ie £154,000 in total). The hostel will not receive Special Needs Management Allowance as its staff - to - resident ratio does not meet the Housing Corporation criteria and because projects which have not received capital funding from the Housing Corporation are not eligible for SNMA.

The Department of Health also gave a grant, direct to Look Ahead Housing Association, to fund initial "start-up" costs prior to the opening of the project in April 1991. This was used principally to fund the employment of staff prior to the opening date.

All parties to this initiative agree that it is vital that sufficient move-on accommodation is made available to residents of the Varden Street Project. As yet no specific funding commitments have been made.

Young single homeless people
Ash Down Hostel, Hendford Hill, Yeovil
South Somerset District Council and Stonham Housing Association

This hostel was opened on 25 June 1990 by Stonham Housing Association.

Stonham's local management committee recognised that existing projects in the area were unable to provide the required level of care and support to young homeless ex-offenders. It approached South Somerset District Council seeking a property to rent and use as a hostel for this client group. South Somerset District Council responded by spending £200,000 on the purchase and renovation of a house in Hendford Hill, Yeovil, which it agreed to lease to Stonham Housing Association.

The house provides temporary accommodation for six young homeless people aged 16 to 20, some of whom are ex-offenders. Most of the young people are referred by the Probation Service and Somerset County Council social services department. They will stay at the hostel for about a year.

There are three project staff (1 full time and 2 part time), one of whom is on duty for most of the day, and there is a call-out system at night for emergencies. This staff team is supported by a relief worker.

The project's aims are:

■ to protect residents while they are still vulnerable

■ to enable residents to learn the practical life skills, normally gained during childhood, needed for independent living

■ to help residents develop the emotional maturity necessary for adult life, such as self esteem and awareness of the consequences of one's actions

■ to assist residents in learning how to amend their behaviour so that they do not commit other offences

■ to help residents to obtain move-on accommodation at the end of their stay (possibly in one of the other Stonham HA projects in Yeovil which provide lower care)

Residents are responsible for most of the shopping, cooking, cleaning and so on. Staff are involved closely with residents, identifying goals and monitoring progress. Counselling services are provided by independent counsellors, funded by grants from local charities.

The hostel receives HDG from the Housing Corporation (and is likely to be switched to SNMA). Top-up funding is mainly provided by Somerset County Council social services department, South Somerset District Council housing department and by the Home Office. However, charitable donations from the Prince's Trust and the Worshipful Company of Weavers have been required to meet a shortfall.

Young people leaving care
Wontner Road 'Floating Support' Scheme
London Borough of Wandsworth and Wandle Housing Association

Wandsworth Independent Living Scheme (WILS) is part of the London Borough of Wandsworth's Department of Social Services and specialises in providing 'floating support' for young people leaving Wandsworth's care facilities. Its staff are part funded by the London Borough of Wandsworth and the Royal Philanthropic Society (which has sponsored a series of projects involving this type of initiative). Day to day management of WILS project has recently been taken over by the Royal Philanthropic Society.

The principal aim of this project is to assist young people leaving care by providing a period of independence training in self contained accommodation owned by either LB Wandsworth or housing associations. If the young people cope successfully they will be nominated for a tenancy of the accommodation they are living in. The Wontner Road project is an example of this work.

This type of initiative is particularly appropriate in the context of the Children's Act 1991. This comes into effect in October 1991 and requires local authorities to prepare young people in their care for the process of leaving it and to provide resources (such as housing) to enable them to do so.

Volunteers befriend the young people and, through regular and committed weekly contact, provide back-up and support. LB Wandsworth social workers liaise closely with volunteers and meet regularly with the young people to look at their general emotional and physical well being. Social workers offer regular counselling to the young people and act as their 'key worker' at times of crisis. WILS scheme workers liaise closely with the volunteers and social workers and are responsible for implementing and monitoring individual training programmes. This entails formal training, in individual or group sessions, in the areas of budgeting, employment, self-care, relationships and property maintenance. WILS scheme workers will also co-ordinate reviews of the progress of each young person and will liaise with housing associations over rent and housing management issues.

The advantage of this type of scheme are that disruptive moves are limited, that the resident's independent housing situation allows flexible support and care to be provided and that a programme of move-on accommodation becomes available to local authority Social Services Departments for children leaving care.

The Wontner Road scheme provides four one-bedroom units for young people leaving care, in two laterally converted properties which also provide two wheelchair units for disabled people on the ground floor.

The revenue funding for Wontner Road project will be provided on a 50/50 basis by London Borough Wandsworth and the Royal Philanthropic Society. Capital funding of £311,000 for acquisition, £302,000 for works and VAT and on costs of £122,00 has been provided entirely by London Borough Wandsworth through the 'Local Authority HAG' mechanism.

A detailed management agreement forms the basis of the partnership and specifies the following responsibilities. WILS scheme staff will manage the accommodation on an agency basis. WILS, not Wandle Housing Association, will decide who the flats are initially allocated to. WILS will take responsibility for rent collection and will guarantee payments to Wandle Housing Association. If the young person does not pay the rent, WILS staff will take the necessary legal steps to seek repossession of the property (with support from Wandle Housing Association). Wandle Housing Association will be responsible for repairs and maintenance.

Wandle Housing Association's special needs housing officer will meet WILS staff on a quarterly basis to review the progress of the project.

Initially, each young person will occupy their flat on an assured shorthold tenancy, drawn up on the basis of the NFHA model. After approximately 12 months, WILS social workers will decide whether the young person is capable of independent living. If they believe so, they will nominate the person for a Wandle Housing Association tenancy of that flat.

If the resident becomes an assured tenant, WILS support will be gradually withdrawn on the basis of mutual agreement between Wandle Housing Association, the social workers and the resident.

The London Borough of Wandsworth has agreed to provide a further £1.5 million for floating support schemes, to be spread over the financial years 1991-2 and 1992-3.

7

LOCAL AUTHORITY SERVICES FOR HOUSING ASSOCIATIONS

Under the Local Authorities (Goods and Services) Act 1970, local authorities are empowered to supply goods and services to other local authorities and public bodies.

The Act specifically empowers local authorities to provide administrative, professional or technical services and to carry out maintenance works in connection with land or buildings.

However, the Act does not extend this power to cover the construction of housing.

Under the Local Authorities (Goods and Services) (Public Bodies) Order 1975 the Secretary of State designated the public bodies covered by the 1970 Act. Included in the definition of 'public bodies' to whom local authorities may supply goods and services are registered housing associations and almshouses.

Example

East London Housing Association - Emergency Repair Service

In 1988 East London Housing Association negotiated an arrangement with the London Borough of Newham whereby the Borough provides the association's tenants with an out-of-hours repairs service.

Before the scheme was developed, the only out-of-office-hours emergency service available to ELHA's 5,000 tenants was the limited make-safe service provided by statutory bodies such as the gas and electricity boards. Under the terms of their tenancy agreement, ELHA tenants could also call out private contractors for other emergencies such as blocked drains. However, under this arrangement ELHA tenants had to pay for work on the spot and claim the outlay back from the association. This clearly presented difficulties for tenants on low incomes. Furthermore, as many of ELHA tenants were elderly, infirm, or disabled they were more likely to have difficulty coping with domestic emergencies.

It was clear that a comprehensive 24 hour emergency service was needed and efforts were made to find a contractor with the necessary wide-ranging building trade skills and organisational back up, operating at prices which could be contained within the general budget provided by the Housing Corporation maintenance allowances. Several commercial contractors were tried but none proved entirely successful. Indeed, one went out of business.

ELHA became aware that under the terms of the Local Authorities (Goods And Services) Act 1970, local authorities could fulfil this role. ELHA approached the London Borough of Newham to see if it would be possible to link ELHA into the major emergency services provided for tenants and residents of the Borough.

ELHA saw that the broad range of the local authority's statutory responsibilities, the scale of its 'in house' maintenance operation and the experience of its direct labour organisation would enable LB Newham to offer a more comprehensive service than any private contractor. For example, the Borough could bring in environmental health officers or structural engineers if circumstances warranted it. In addition, the Borough was already operating a 24-hour emergency service for its own tenants and always had large supplies of raw materials in store.

Meetings took place between officers of both organisations and it was agreed that LB Newham's staff would deal directly with ELHA tenants and that their tradespeople would attend to ELHA properties even when they were outside Newham's boundaries. As ELHA properties were also located in the Boroughs of Redbridge, Barking, Dagenham and Tower Hamlets this represented a significant change in working practice for LB Newham employees. However, after local negotiations with trade unions, arrangements were agreed.

The out-of-hours service was to apply only to emergency works and ELHA and LB Newham agreed on common definitions of an emergency, appropriate response times and the schedule of charges to be applied. Contractual arrangements, including a schedule of rates, are fixed on an annual basis with both organisations being able to terminate the relationship at the year end. ELHA agreed to guarantee LB Newham employees a minimum of one hour's pay per call-out, regardless of how much time the work actually took. Borough employees confine their works to 'patch repairs' with ELHA retaining responsibility for long term remedial works. If patch repairs are inappropriate, as in the case of heating or sanitary facilities for example, LB Newham employees can supply portable space heaters or chemical toilets from their stores. In the event of uncertainty, LB Newham's emergency maintenance control centre contacts ELHA's maintenance manager for advice or authorisation.

To enable LB Newham employees to verify that a householder is an ELHA tenant, lists of ELHA's properties, tenants and rent account numbers have been loaded directly onto the Newham Building Services computer. Each month, ELHA sends the Borough an update of this information.

Finally, a Cellnet telephone was purchased by ELHA and its 'divert facility' is used to link emergency calls into Newham's maintenance control centre. This means that the emergency number issued to ELHA tenants in their handbook will never need to be changed and that calls can be diverted to another number should the LB Newham service be changed or discontinued.

Quality control by ELHA is maintained by treating LB Newham in the same way as any other contractor. A random sample of twenty jobs per contractor, valued at under £200, are inspected by ELHA maintenance and housing officers per month. Any complaints received lead to automatic inspection. All jobs valued at more than £200 are also automatically inspected by ELHA maintenance officers.

Since the scheme came into effect in June 1988, around 350 out-of-hours emergency call outs from ELHA tenants have been dealt with by Newham Building Services at an average of 15 per month with an average cost of £31 a job. The system has worked very effectively.

Example

Royal Borough of Kensington and Chelsea 'Community Alarm System'

The Royal Borough's Directorate of Housing and Property Services operates a community alarm system for its elderly and people who are disabled and extends the service to tenants of local housing associations.

The community alarm is a telephone unit which automatically dials a Control Centre when activated by a user who requires medical assistance or other forms of help. The Control Centre is staffed by RB Kensington and Chelsea personnel, 24 hours per day on every day of the year.

In an emergency, the user activates the alarm by pressing a button on the unit or another button located in a pendant, which contains a radio transmitter and can be worn around the neck. As soon as the call reaches the Control Centre, details of the caller appear on a computer screen. These details will include the caller's name and address, medical history, whether keys are held by the Control Centre, the name of their doctor, and information on how to contact someone who can let the emergency services enter the user's home in order to provide help.

The telephone unit has a built in loudspeaker and a microphone. This enables Control Centre staff to talk to the user and to hear their replies. The technology is sophisticated enough to permit this dialogue to take place even if the user is not in the room where the telephone unit is located. The unit can be used in conjunction with smoke detectors, intruder alarms and thermal alarms.

Local housing associations who use the RB Kensington and Chelsea Community Alarm include Carib Housing Association (which specifically houses elderly Afro-Caribbean people), Kensington Housing Trust, Notting Hill Housing Trust, Octavia Hill Housing Trust, Peabody Trust, Samuel Lewis Housing Trust, Servite Housing Association, Shepherds Bush Housing Association, Sutton Housing Association and the Womens Pioneer Housing Trust.

Tenants 'opt in' to the Community Alarm system on an individual basis. They can choose to buy or rent the telephone unit from the Royal Borough. They can choose to 'buy into' a mobile warden service, which means that a warden personally visits to assist in an emergency. The cost of the service is defrayed by charges which are passed onto the tenant in the form of a small weekly service charge, for which Housing Benefit can be claimed.

The advantage to the housing association is that their tenants receive emergency support without any of the capital or revenue outlay which would be required were the association to operate its own emergency Control Centre. The system can be used for sheltered schemes on a 'out-of-hours' basis or for people who live independently on a '24 hour' basis.

The Control Centre can also operate, out of hours, controlled door entry for a sheltered with a speech link to the speaker at the main entrance door.

This approach is recommended by the charity Help The Aged.

8

NOMINATION AGREEMENTS

The purpose of this chapter is to explain:

■ recent policy recommendations about nomination agreements between local authorities and housing associations

■ some of the important issues related to these agreements

■ methods of improving nomination procedures

■ methods of improving liaison between local authorities and housing associations with regard to nominations

Policy recommendations regarding nomination agreements

It is the policy of the current government to direct capital resources for social housing towards housing associations rather than local authorities. However, local authorities will retain their existing statutory obligation to secure housing for certain categories of homeless people.

As the impact of this policy develops, local authorities will increasingly rely upon nominations to housing associations to fulfil these statutory obligations towards homeless people and, indeed, to rehouse applicants from their waiting and transfer lists.

This makes the implementation of nomination agreements a critical area of local authority and housing association partnership.

In recent years there have been several important statements on the nominations issue.

Housing Corporation Circular 48/89 urged associations to honour existing nomination arrangements and to increase the assistance they offer local authorities in housing homeless people. The circular pointed out that under Section 72 of the Housing Act 1985, a local authority can require housing associations to provide it with 'reasonable assistance' in meeting its responsibilities to homeless people.

The National Federation of Housing Associations, the Association of Metropolitan Authorities and the Association of District Councils have agreed a joint statement on local authority nominations to housing associations.
It recommends that:

■ authorities and associations should establish targets for the percentage of nominations going to homeless people

■ that joint definitions of 'homelessness' should be agreed, and that associations should work together to overcome any 'lack of fit' between the size of the housing stock that they can make available and the authority's need for family sized accommodation.

Similar arrangements have been agreed in Wales, involving the Welsh Federation of Housing associations, Tai Cymru and the Council of Welsh Districts.

However, the most useful guidance on the detailed implementation of nomination agreements is contained in 'Partners In Meeting Housing Need', a highly authoritative publication produced by the Association of London Authorities, the London Boroughs Association, the London Housing Associations Council and published by the National Federation of Housing Associations.

This publication is recommended reading, and its principal recommendations are included in this chapter, together with many supplementary observations.

Key Policy Issues

A number of policy issues need to be tackled when nomination agreements are being developed.

Nominations as a percentage of lettings

The standard set by the Housing Corporation in its Circular 48/89 states that 50% of all lettings in schemes funded by the Corporation should be made to local authority nominees.

Given the changed distribution of capital resources between authorities and associations and the ever rising number of statutory homeless households, the standard demanded by Housing Corporation Circular 48/89 now seems too low.

Fortunately, housing associations are free to agree to local authority proposals for higher levels of nominations. Provided that the Housing Corporation is sure that there has been no coercion involved on the part of the local authority, it is unlikely to intervene.

In Wales, Tai Cymru allows local authorities and housing associations to reach agreement on nomination levels without the need for its approval provided that the nominations fall within the following guidelines - 50% where there is no input of local authority land or finance into the development, 100% where there is no Tai Cymru funding input and 75% where the local authority and Tai Cymru provide a similar level of subsidy towards the development.

In practice, the 50% figure has tended to be minimum rather than a maximum. In London, it has become common on HAG funded schemes for 75% of initial lettings (on family sized units of two bedrooms and above) and 50% of relets to go to local authority nominees.

Where local authorities have sold land to housing associations, even higher nomination levels are common. Indeed, when giving consent for the sale of local authority land to housing associations, the DoE has agreed that 100% nomination arrangements are acceptable provided that the initiative is targeted at homeless households and as long as arrangements for relets revert back to 50% after a 10 year period.

The DoE has also stipulated that 100% of housing association lettings funded under its recent 'homelessness initiative' must be used for statutory homeless households nominated by local authorities.

Which Lettings Are Taken Into Account?

It is now generally accepted that associations should make a fair selection of vacancies (by size, type, age and location) available to local authority nominees.

As Housing Corporation Circular 48/89 points out:

"It is not reasonable for associations to make available for local authority nominations only a percentage of its residual vacancies, after all the desirable ones have been used for internal transfers".

Yet there is concern amongst local authorities that some associations are carrying out internal transfers before stating their available voids and that the number of family sized units being made available to the authority is thus correspondingly, and unfairly, reduced.

On the other hand, housing associations have argued that it is consistent with the terms of the Housing Corporation's 'Tenants' Guarantee' for their existing tenants to have reasonable transfer opportunities and that a significant proportion of the family sized units available to the association for reletting must be made available for transfers.

This issue can only be resolved by mutual agreement at a local level. The following recommendations are made in 'Partners In Meeting Housing Need'.

Transfers or exchanges which involve the association in a reciprocal obligation and decants where the tenant intends to return should be 'netted off' before the number of 'true voids' is determined.

The definition of a 'true void' should be one where a 'net gain' of accommodation becomes available to a housing association. Thus a 'true void' will include every letting becoming available on new developments and every relet which is not 'netted off' on the terms stated above.

By defining the void according to the status of the departing tenant, objective criteria for determining a 'fair cross section of lettings' are introduced.

Housing associations should, thereafter, supply the local authority with annual details of all their lettings (including information on bedroom size) to verify that the agreed definition of a 'true void' is being upheld and that a fair spread of properties has been offered to the authority.

In practice, the recommended method would work as follows.

The first call on housing association vacancies would normally be decants, reciprocal transfers and 'priority need' transfers. Of the remaining voids, 75% of family sized dwellings and 50% of smaller units would be made available to local authority nominees. Housing associations would then be able to use the remaining 25% of family sized units and 50% of smaller units to house special project nominees and people from their own waiting and transfer lists.

Defining A Homeless Household

It seems reasonable that, as local authorities have the duty of assessing applications from homeless people, associations should abide by decisions of local authorities on which households are statutorily homeless and which are not.

Overcoming the mismatch between need and property characteristics

Another policy issue concerns ways of overcoming the mismatch between the size and nature of housing association dwellings and the requirements of local authority nominees.

Associations which have developed a large number of units suitable for single people will clearly be ill equipped to house homeless families. It would also be unwise, for example, to expect an association specialising in housing for elderly people to suddenly take responsibility for other types of household.

Associations with a preponderance of smaller units may need to accept some nominations of under-occupying (rather than homeless) local authority tenants in order to free up family sized local authority stock.

Associations may also wish to consider a similar rationalisation of their own stock by making maximum use of the Tenant Incentive Scheme - where the Housing Corporation funds 'portable discounts' to assist tenants to buy private sector property.

Associations may also need to act in concert to ensure that each one makes a specific contribution towards the needs of homeless households. This may involve, for instance, associations which predominantly own primarily family sized stock responding to transfer requests from small households by offering transfers to other local associations whose stock consists predominantly of smaller units. This would, in turn, free up larger units in the stock of the 'exporting' housing association which could then be made available to homeless households nominated by the local authority.

Whilst these policy changes will result in some loss of flexibility and independence on the part of housing associations, there is no real alternative if the current homelessness crisis is to be tackled. However, it may be difficult to persuade local authority tenants to switch tenures if housing association rents are significantly higher than those charged by the authority. It may also be difficult persuading any tenant to move where this involves a switch from a secure to an assured tenancy.

Maximising the number of homeless households that are nominated

Local authorities will need to increase the proportion of homeless households who are nominees. Research conducted for the 'Partners' publication found that in London - where pressure of homelessness is greatest - "some boroughs with large numbers of households in temporary accommodation appeared not to be making the most effective use of nominations to house homeless people" and that "three boroughs nominated no homeless households whatsoever".

Improving Nomination Procedures

Whilst local authorities have sought to improve the number and quality of nominations obtained to housing association property, associations have raised valid complaints that procedural problems at the local authority end have often restricted the take-up of those nominations that have been available.

Again, effective working arrangements will only be maintained by agreement at a local level based upon a mutual understanding by authorities and associations of each others objectives and difficulties.

Demand for nominations must not be restricted by faulty procedures.

The first task is to ensure that people in housing need do not refuse nominations because they are unaware or misinformed about the nature of housing associations or because they cannot understand the nominations procedure.

'Partners' recommends that local authorities should make a leaflet about housing associations available to all applicants for local authority housing. The leaflet would explain what housing associations are, which ones operate in the borough and so on. The leaflet should be translated into languages appropriate for all of the residents of the local authority concerned. A model leaflet is supplied in 'Partners'.

'Partners' recommends that local authority application forms ask applicants whether they would consider nomination to a housing association and explain how the nomination process works.

If tenants are willing to be nominated, they should be supplied with a nomination form which contains all the information required by associations prior to letting a property. It will be helpful if all associations working within a local authority area standardise their information requirements as much as possible. 'Partners' supplies a model nomination form.

Choosing the appropriate nominations method

The second task is to develop an effective method of nominating households.

There is evidence that nominating one individual for each available property is costly and inefficient. If the nominee rejects the offer or simply doesn't turn up, the nominations process slows down, the property remains void and the association faces loss of rent.

'Partners' recommends the nomination of a batch of applicants for each property, numbered in order of priority. This will enable further nominees to view the property quickly if the first nominee turns it down. This is known as the 'prioritised batch system'.

However, 'Partners' acknowledges that for letting bedsits, one bedroom units, sheltered housing units and shared housing schemes, it may be more effective for the local authority to combine the 'prioritised batch system' with a pool of nominees which can be drawn upon as and when properties become available.

Common definitions of housing need

It is essential that local authorities and housing associations agree a common definition of priority need. 'Partners' argues that local authorities should prioritise homeless households and under-occupying council tenants whose transfer will release a family sized unit. 'Partners' argues that associations should accept the local authority's definition of 'priority need'.

This means that associations may need to be more flexible about matters such as residence or income qualifications than hitherto. Equally, local authorities should consult local housing associations when determining their 'acceptance', 'intentionality' and 'number of offer' policies with regard to homeless applicants. Housing associations are unlikely to be keen to extend nomination arrangements if they feel that acceptance and offer policies are unfair.

Whilst housing associations must retain their right to refuse nominations, this should only be exercised in exceptional cases and then only on the ground of unsuitability of a particular property for the nominee and not because of perceived future management problems.

Avoidance Of Direct And Indirect Discrimination

Authorities and associations should examine their allocations practices for evidence of any form of direct or indirect discrimination and each party should be satisfied that the other has taken steps necessary to eliminate it. Detailed advice on this subject is available in the 'Partners' publication.

Time Limits

To ensure speedy take-up of nominations and reduce association vulnerability to rent loss, time limits should be set for every stage of the nomination process. Again, 'Partners' provides detailed guidelines on this matter.

However, these time limits should be applied sensitively. For example, some local authorities make only one offer of accommodation to homeless households. In such cases, the authority is likely to consider that it has discharged its statutory obligation if an applicant, who has been nominated to a housing association property, rejects the offer. It will therefore be helpful to applicants if housing associations 'hold open' offers of accommodation for two or three days after refusal, to allow an applicant to reconsider their decision in the light of the local authority's response.

Mutual Exchanges

Finally, authorities and associations need to develop an integrated local system for dealing with mutual exchanges. This should be done in consultation with the national mobility organisation, HOMES, which assists local authorities and housing associations.

Improved Liaison

The following steps can be taken to improve liaison between local authorities and housing associations over the issue of nominations.

Monitoring The Progress Of Agreements

Regular monitoring is essential if the effectiveness of nomination arrangements is to be assessed. Monitoring will not only involve matters such as take-up, refusals and unsuccessful nominations, but will deal with the important question of equal opportunities. Gender and ethnic monitoring of nominations, allocations and quality of accommodation offered is required. 'Partners' recommends that all parties adopt its suggested 'quality of accommodation' criteria and the definition of ethnicity contained in the NFHA CORE returns.

Nomination arrangements should be standing items on the agendas of local authority/housing association 'liaison groups'. Where such groups do not exist, they should be set up as soon as possible and all associations operating with the borough should be encouraged to attend.

Joint training should be available for all authority and association staff who are involved with allocations.

Specific Liaison Officers

'Partners' recommends that local authorities should nominate at least one officer to be responsible for liaison with housing associations. The officer should have sufficient experience and seniority to be able to do that job effectively. Each association should, on the same basis, nominate at least one officer to be responsible for liaison with the local authority.

Harmonising Local Authority Procedures

A particular problem for housing associations operating in several local authority areas in that different authorities will have different policies and procedures. This will inhibit the association's efficiency and is a strong argument for neighbouring authorities to establish consistent practices where possible. There is an important role for both IOH and NFHA Regional officers in stimulating consistent practice.

Example

London Borough of Lewisham Nominations Agreement

This agreement represents a procedure for operating the nominations process for all Associations working within the London Borough of Lewisham.

It covers first lets and relets on the following types of schemes:

- Consortium new-build general needs
- Consortium new-build shared ownership
- Consortium new-build co-op schemes
- Consortium new-build special needs schemes
- Corporation funded schemes (other than Consortium schemes)
- Borough funded schemes
- Borough funded major repair schemes

The calculation of a nomination should be undertaken using the definition of a void given below.

All housing associations working in Lewisham are requested to become signatories to this Agreement.

Progress with the implementation of the Agreement will be monitored through completion of a quarterly monitoring form by housing associations and will be discussed at quarterly meetings between individual Associations and Borough liaison officers. A summary of progress will be reported to every London Housing Associations Liaison Group (LEWHAG) meeting.

The terms and conditions of the agreement will be reviewed on an annual basis by the Borough and LEWHAG.

Consortium New-Build schemes

These refer to schemes where approved Associations have been given Housing Corporation funding to develop land which has been purchased from the council.

- General Needs Schemes First lettings - 75% Re-lets - 50%
- Shared Ownership schemes Nominations rights - 50%
- Co-op Schemes First lettings - 50% Re-lets - 50%
- Special Needs Schemes

Individual referral rights will be negotiated with the council's Special Housing Group and agreed by letter by the Chair and Vice-Chair of the council's housing committee.

Corporation funded schemes

These refer to schemes which have been funded by the Corporation outside the consortium arrangement and apply to both general needs and special needs projects.
First lettings - 50% Re-lets - 50%
This will be the minimum level of nominations accepted by the local authority. Higher levels of nominations may be negotiated on individual schemes if the Association wishes to assist a particular Borough need eg homelessness, sheltered accommodation.

All re-lets will be subject to the local authority obtaining 25% true voids for 1-bed units, 75% true voids for 2-bed units and 50% true voids for 3-bed units.

Borough funded schemes

These are schemes funded by the council.

It is envisaged that support will have taken place from a particular circumstance - eg favourable disposal of council-owned land or properties - therefore nominations above 50% on first lettings will be expected.

Borough funded major repair schemes

These are schemes where either the Borough or the GLC has been the original funder and they now require major repairs to bring them up to acceptable modern day standards. In return for supporting their funding, the Borough has negotiated the following nomination levels:
First lettings - 100% - except where there are decant cases who are returning.
Re-lets - 100%

Defination of a true void

'Partners In Meeting Housing Need' states that a local authority and housing associations need to agree a common definition of a 'true void' and use this for monitoring purposes.

It is recommended that all housing associations working in Lewisham adopt the definition preferred by the ALA/LHAC/LBA group (and recommended in 'Partners In Meeting Housing Need').

This method ensures that the Borough obtains a fair proportion of lettings of all sizes. True voids should be defined as:

■ Voids within new-build or newly rehabilitated schemes.

■ Voids created through tenant moves to another landlord where no reciprocal arrangement exists

■ Voids created by the death of the tenant where there is no statutory right to succession

■ Voids created by tenants buying their own property in the private sector

■ Voids created by eviction or abandonment of property

■ Non-priority transfers (only priority transfers should be netted off)

The definition of a priority transfer is:

■ Urgent medical cases

■ Racial or sexual harassment and domestic violence

■ Statutory overcrowding which is defined as 2+ people too many for bedroom size

■ Accommodation is structurally unsound

■ Under-occupation where it frees priority sized accommodation

■ Decants

It is noted that all vacancies occurring because of the Tenant Incentive Scheme should be treated as a nomination to the local authority and should be targeted towards the homeless.

Example

Royal Borough of Kensington and Chelsea Nomination Agreement

The agreement applies to all housing association properties funded by the Royal Borough of Kensington and Chelsea and also includes those inside the Borough where development was funded by other sources.

Housing association properties located outside the Borough are subject to the Agreement if their development was funded by the Royal Borough of Kensington and Chelsea.

Hostels and short-life property are exempt from the Agreement.

The calculation of the Borough's entitlement is based on the reason a property becomes void.

Voids fall into two categories:

■ True Voids of which the Borough receives 50% (unless a different percentage has previously been negotiated)

■ Non-True Voids to which the Borough has no entitlement

Operating The Agreement

First the association should decide if it requires the void for letting to a decant case. If the answer is yes the association has first call on the property.

If the property is not required for letting to a decant the association should look at the reason why the dwelling was vacated in the first instance and, using the following definitions, decide whether it is a TRUE or NON-TRUE VOID.

Definition of a True Void - to which the Borough has a 50% entitlement

■ Voids within new build or rehab schemes ie first lettings

■ Voids created through tenant moves to other landlords where no reciprocal commitment exists

■ Voids created by death of a tenant where there is no statutory right of succession

■ Voids created by a tenant buying their own property

■ Voids created by abandonment of tenancy or eviction

■ Voids created by rehousing of permanent decant

■ Voids created by temporary decant returning to former home

Definition of a Non-True Void - to which the Borough has no entitlement

■ Voids created by a temporary decant moving to temporary home

■ Voids created through tenant transfers within the association's stock

■ Voids created through reciprocal arrangements and moves via the Housing Association HOMES scheme

Allocation of True Voids to the Borough

If the property is a TRUE VOID the Borough should receive every second TRUE VOID in strict sequence. This should ensure a 50% entitlement and a cross section of different dwelling types and sizes during each financial year. If an association has a specific need for a TRUE VOID which should go to the Borough, they should consult with the Borough.

If the property is a NON-TRUE VOID the association has no obligation to offer it to the Borough.

If associations wish to replace a TRUE VOID with a NON-TRUE VOID they must consult the Borough.

In order to assist the Borough with family units for the homeless, associations may wish to negotiate a higher percentage of TRUE VOIDS to go to the Borough.

Monitoring The Agreement

Associations are required to complete 'Void Quarterly Monitoring Returns'.

Associations must be specific in completing the 'Reason For Void' column ie state the reason why a property became void. Terms such as 'relet', 'casual vacancy' and 'unknown' make the exercise and the spirit of the Nominations Agreement invalid.

The Borough will send reminders to associations if returns are not completed.

If it is evident from the returns that the association has misinterpreted the Agreement or built up a TRUE VOID debt, the Borough will discuss this with the association.

From time to time, to monitor the Nominations Agreement, the Borough will organise a lettings audit as undertaken by the London Research Centre in 1989.

Example

London Housing Unit 'Model' Nominations Agreement

In December 1990, the London Housing Unit published a model nominations agreement for rented units of accommodation. Its content represents a development of the recommendations of 'Partners In Housing Need'. The document is available from the London Housing Unit, Bedford House, 125-133 Camden High Street, London NW1 7JR (Tel. 071 284 3154) priced £2.

9

JOINT TRAINING INITIATIVES

The purpose of this chapter is to outline:
- the nature and benefits of co-ordinated staff training
- the benefits to local authorities and housing associations of undertaking joint training initiatives

Training Requirements

Both local authority and housing association staff require different levels of training. Decision makers will require ideas for changing their organisations and assistance in defining the tasks that their staff will need to undertake. The (larger numbers of) staff employed to implement these decisions will require task-based skills training.

Organisations in both sectors will also require different types of training. There will be a continuing need, at all levels of an organisation, for personal development training on matters such as assertiveness, public speaking, career development and so on. Similarly, there will be an ongoing need for skills development training on matters such as implementing equal opportunities, letter writing, report writing, interviewing, dealing with aggressive clients, assisting tenants to participate in decision making and so on. There will be a regular but less frequent need at all staff levels for knowledge development training on issues such as new legislation, new procedures and so on. There will be a recurring need (mainly for managerial staff) for policy development training on issues such as local authority/housing association partnership initiatives, equal opportunities policies, tenant participation policies and so on.

Finally, there is a need for management training for senior staff. Many housing organisations promote staff to management positions, on the basis of their success in the technical aspects of their current posts, without first training them in the skills of staff and organisational management. In a period of major change and upheaval following the 1988 and 1989 housing legislation, management skills are of particular importance to local authorities and housing associations.

Training Budgets

Many housing organisations do not have an identified training budget, which means that training is especially vulnerable if economies have to be made. There is also evidence that the amount of money being spent on staff training is inadequate, particularly at a time of great change in social housing. A recent DoE study 'Training, Education and Performance In Housing Management' found that some local authorities and housing associations were spending less than 1% of their annual budget on staff training. If this figure is compared to the Confederation of British Industry recommendation to employers that they should spend 5% of their overall budget on staff training, coupled with the Audit Commission's endorsement of the 8% spent annually by the Metropolitan Police, it appears that housing staff are being under-trained.

Assessing And Meeting Training Needs

It is fundamentally important that before housing organisations commit money and staff time to training that they identify the precise training needs of their staff and the appropriate training opportunities that are available to meet these needs.

This time consuming but necessary process can be achieved by housing organisations through a formal, and ongoing, training needs analysis.

The training needs analysis would identify which staff need what type of training, which external courses are relevant for particular staff and what scope exists for in-house training. The analysis would also identify the organisation's training needs, for example regarding the staff training required to change the organisation's culture to enable it to adapt to change. In housing associations, for instance, a greater degree of entrepreneurial aptitude may be required to respond to new development opportunities, minimise financial risk and attract private finance. For some local authorities, an increased emphasis on customer care may be required. For those authorities which are currently considering large scale voluntary transfer, training on the culture and modes of operation of housing associations will clearly be relevant.

The training needs analysis will thus enable organisations to develop a coherent training strategy as opposed to the ad-hoc approach that is often adopted in practice. The organisation might, for instance, decide to adopt the concept of 'linked career grades'. For example, housing officers would be appointed on (say) Scale 4 but could progress to Scale 6 (with consequent salary increases) whilst staying in the same post. However, movement up the scale would be dependent upon the successful completion of specific training in addition to the normal requirement of on-the-job experience. The training would be linked to the core tasks that the postholder is required to undertake.

For example, a local authority housing department or large association might commission a training agency to undertake the in-house training of all its housing officers in housing law. The training might take place over a year, might be based on case studies which relate to the organisation's own experience and might lead to a certificate of competence at the end of the process.

The idea of standards of competence is particularly relevant because housing authorities are now required to publish Performance Indicators related to managerial efficiency and quality of services and housing associations are being required to meet Housing Corporation Performance Expectations. If these overall standards are to be achieved, all housing organisations need to ensure that the component parts of that service (and the postholders who provide the services) operate efficiently. Indeed, the new National Vocational Qualification (NVQ) aims to set standards of competence and to measure staff performance against these standards. The NVQ might well form a key element of meeting the training needs identified in the analysis.

An authoritative training needs analysis will also assist Directors of local authority housing departments and Directors/Chief Executives of housing associations in obtaining committee approval for adequate levels of expenditure on training.

Role of Professional Training Managers

In many local authorities and housing associations, responsibility for training is given to middle managers who have neither professional experience or qualifications in training and who have a substantial existing workload which is unrelated to training. This assignment of responsibility reflects both the low priority often given to staff training and the lack of understanding of the benefits which can be obtained by employing professional training managers.

Professional training managers can maximise the effectiveness of sector based and joint training by applying the following skills:

- realism about what can be achieved on one or two days training

- developing a training needs analysis - identifying needs in consultation with the staff involved

- identifying the most (cost) effective methods of meeting particular training needs

- designing in-house training through the development of stimulating methods of presenting information and through intensive briefing of trainers regarding the needs of staff

At present, there are very few professional training organisers in the housing movement. Changing this situation will require a commitment to major investment in terms of appropriate salaries and/or vocational training for existing staff.

Small associations, which cannot afford to employ a specialist training manager, should place responsibility for training with a member of staff no lower than 'second tier' and should ensure that the person receives the training required to exercise this function effectively. The Institute of Housing provides training on how to manage training functions and budgets, in addition to courses providing 'skills training for trainers'.

Benefits Of Joint Training Initiatives

Where joint training is provided, particularly in policy development, lateral thinking and contact building can lead to closer relationships between associations and authorities which may provide a direct stimulus to new partnerships.

Individual organisations often cannot get value for money from technological aids unless they share their use with other bodies. An example is closed circuit television, which is essential for 'interpersonal skills training' in areas such as customer relations, staff coaching and appraisal, negotiating and liaison skills.

Joint training can stimulate a better understanding of the problems faced by staff in other housing sectors by breaking down the misconceptions which create psychological barriers which, in turn, inhibit effective partnerships. For example, many associations could benefit from a clearer understanding of the resource constraints which local authorities operate under and many authorities could benefit from a better appreciation of the problems experienced by housing associations since the introduction of 'mixed funding'. Other areas where joint training can stimulate better understanding are rent arrears recovery and housing benefit, nominations and special needs housing.

Lack of understanding of the financial regime and management styles operating in the other sector has inhibited the ability of staff to move between sectors. A better understanding of these issues will increase the pool of recruitable staff for both authorities and associations.

The skills and understanding of trainers are also enhanced by having to cover issues in ways which are relevant to staff of both sectors. In particular, trainers are able to give information on local authority 'good practice' to housing association staff and vice versa.

Examples of Joint Training Initiatives

Cumbria Housing Training Group

The Cumbria Housing Training Group was set up in 1982 as a joint initiative between local authorities and housing associations in the county. The main aim of the Group is to arrange an annual programme of training events to meet needs identified by member organisations. Its member organisations include Allerdale District Council, Anchor Housing Association, Barrow Borough Council, Carlisle City Council, Copeland Borough Council, Eden District Council, Impact Housing Association, North Housing Association, South Lakeland District Council and Two Castles Housing Association. Each of these organisations has appointed a training co-ordinator from their staff to sit on the Group's steering committee. The Group employs a part-time professional training organiser.

Since 1989, the Group has published a bi-annual Newsletter which reports on its work and on other social housing developments in the county. Copies are distributed to all staff and committee members of the member organisations. A recent issue included features on 'The Housing Corporation Cash Crisis - The Cumbrian Dimension', new local authority and housing association appointments and developments regarding National Vocational Qualifications and the Institute of Housing professional qualification.

One of the Group's specific aims is for local authority and housing association staff to share information and learn from each other. To achieve this, the Group undertakes joint training courses and has compiled a network of contacts to enable the training co-ordinators of member organisations to run in-house courses.

There is an annual subscription charge of £300 (£200 for small associations) which provides a working balance, supports production of the newsletter, and ensures that training events can be offered at competitive rates.

Once the Group has finalised its annual training programme, individual member organisations take responsibility for organising specific events. In this way, the group is able to operate with minimal overheads and admin support.

In 1990, with the help of the Cumbria Housing Group and the Cumbria Rural Housing Group, the Training Group organised the first Cumbria Housing Conference. Over 70 delegates attended from housing associations, parish councils, district council housing and planning departments and building societies. The theme of the conference was 'Affordable Homes For Cumbria' and speakers included Housing Corporation and DoE staff, a planning consultant and the Anglican Archdeacon of Westmorland and Furness.

The Group's annual training programme for 1991 includes 20 courses covering subjects such as housing management performance indicators, housing benefit, understanding housing policy, the Children's Act and family law, 'homelessness - the new Code of Guidance' and a members seminar targeted at local authority housing committee and housing association management committee members.

North East Housing Associations' Training Group

The North East Housing Associations' Training Group represents 44 housing associations in the North East region. It provides a wide variety of training programmes in professional and personal development for all staff and committee members of housing associations. It employs three staff on the basis of revenue funding obtained from subscriptions from its member associations and a Housing Corporation grant. Training is provided to non member housing organisations at a higher rate than members are charged.

The North East Housing Associations Training Group has recognised the cumulative impact of the Housing Act 1988 and the Local Government and Housing Act 1989 - in particular the government's definition of housing associations as the primary 'providers' of new social housing and the local authorities as 'enablers'. The Group states that:

"The provision of social housing depends now to a great extent on local authorities and housing associations approaching the problem from a corporate standpoint."

In recognition of a growing need for closer links and greater understanding between these two partners the Group has recently past year taken three specific initiatives.

In May 1990, the Group organised a one-day conference for Directors, Chief Executives and Housing Directors of local authorities and housing associations operating in the region, entitled "The Future Of Social Housing In The 1990's: Survival Or Growth?" Around 40 delegates attended, evenly split between local authority and housing association staff. Sessions covered issues such as raising private finance, authority/association development partnerships, performance indicators and tenant participation. Speakers included a housing finance consultant, the Director of a voluntary nightshelter (who was also the Lord Mayor of Leeds at the time) and the Head of Housing Research and Policy at Sheffield City Council.

In October 1990, in association with the Institute of Housing, the Group organised a course entitled "Local Authorities And Housing Associations: Working Together" for senior staff and committee members of both types of organisation. Again, around 40 delegates attended, evenly split between local authority and housing association representatives. Speakers from the Institute of Housing covered topics such as the new financial regime for local authorities, planning and land availability, the sale of local authority land to housing associations, stock transfer and nomination agreements.

Feedback from these courses indicated a desire for further day-long joint training events concentrating on each of the following subjects:

■ joint training issues

■ tackling homelessness

■ rent setting and affordability

■ housing benefit payments

■ land deals

■ housing finance

■ nomination procedures

During 1991 and 1992, the Group will be arranging joint training courses to meet this demand.

In its third initiative, the Group is planning to run a series of programmes on 'Care In The Community And Homelessness' which will involve housing association, local authority, health authority and voluntary group staff as speakers and delegates.

Institute Of Housing (Northern Regional Office)

The Institute of Housing's Northern Regional Office (NRO) was opened in Leeds in March 1988 to provide comprehensive training, information and membership services to local authorities and housing associations in the Northern region. The NRO employs four experienced trainers/managers to co-ordinate and teach its training programme. The NRO provides training and consultancy services on organisational development, policy development, finance, customer service and skills development.

The NRO is gearing the bulk of its training towards a mixed audience. The IOH NRO has provides 'marketed' training courses and 'in house' training days tailored to the specific needs of housing associations, local authorities, housing association training schemes or local joint training groups. The bulk of the 'marketed' training courses are designed to accommodate staff from both local authorities and housing associations. All courses have been specially devised to be relevant to both local authority and housing association staff.

To ensure that it meets the needs of these organisations effectively, the NRO has set up a Training Advisory Board. The Board is composed of representatives from individual local authorities and housing associations, the National Federation of Housing Associations, the Association of Metropolitan Authorities and the Department of the Environment. The Board advises the NRO on the specific training needs of both sectors, provides feedback on the quality of training provided and generally offers objective external monitoring of the NRO's work.

The Institute also offers a free advice service to other housing or training organisations which wish to develop training on housing issues. This advice will cover methods of training, key issues and information on the range of available courses and trainers for both sector based and joint training.

Also worthy of note is the contribution of the Institute's 12 regional branches which cover England, Scotland, Wales and Northern Ireland. Branch activity is organised on a voluntary basis by IOH members belong to both authorities and associations. Activities include newsletters, joint conferences and discussion forums, are primarily held in the evenings and provide an important opportunity for staff from authorities and associations to 'network' and share ideas.

10

HOUSING BENEFIT PAYMENTS

The purpose of this chapter is to outline:
- the importance of housing benefit payments to housing associations and their tenants
- the reasons why problems with housing benefit payment occur
- practical steps which local authorities and housing associations can take to improve both the 'take up' of housing benefit and the efficiency of benefit payment itself

Importance of Housing Benefit to Housing Associations and their tenants

Around 65% of housing association tenants are entitled to receive housing benefit from their local authority. The NFHA estimates that only around 50% of association tenants are currently in receipt of housing benefit, indicating that 15% of tenants are not taking up their entitlement.

Housing benefit is very important in terms of the ability of housing association tenants to pay their rent. Underpayment, overpayment and delays in benefit payment all raise the prospect of rent arrears and tenant anxiety. The importance of this issue has been demonstrated by Glasgow University research which found that 51% of housing association tenant arrears could be attributed to the effect of reduced housing benefit or delays in housing benefit payment.

The flow of housing benefit payments has a major impact on the cashflow of housing associations themselves. Any delay in benefit payment will upset an association's financial planning. Given the complexity of the benefit system and frequent disputes about the precise level of benefit entitlement, it may also be difficult for associations to predict the amount of rent arrears which will be recoverable. Small housing associations are particularly vulnerable to these cash flow problems.

Delayed payment also leads to the loss of interest on revenue balances, which may inhibit the ability of associations to employ new staff or to subsidise rents on new developments. One London association, for example, suffered lost interest amounting to £30,000 in 1990-1 due solely to delays in the payment of housing benefit.

Chasing rent arrears is a major element of the work of housing management staff in every association. The time consuming nature of this task is compounded where housing officers have to assist tenants in resolving their benefit problems.

Delays and uncertainty over housing benefit payment can also make it difficult for associations to implement housing management policies fairly. It is normal for associations, as with local authorities, to restrict a tenant's eligibility for a transfer, an exchange or a Tenant Incentive Scheme move if they are in rent arrears. However, if the arrears are solely attributable to delays in housing benefit payment such sanctions are clearly unfair. Association staff often have great difficulty determining whether arrears are due to late benefit payment or are, indeed, due to non payment by the tenant.

Tenants' security of tenure can also be affected by housing benefit payments. The vast majority of housing associations have clear procedures regarding the eviction of tenants who do not pay their rent. These procedures allow tenants several opportunities to clear their arrears or make formal agreements to do so, before each stage of the possession and eviction procedure is triggered. However, associations are caught in a difficult position where disputes about housing benefit payment occur. Associations can either believe the tenant's testimony and risk irrecoverable arrears if they are wrong, or disregard the tenant's evidence and invoke possession proceedings unfairly.

Key Areas of the Housing Benefit Process

The following factors are of particular importance where the effectiveness of the housing benefit system is being considered.

Assessment of Benefit Entitlement

Housing association tenants are classed as 'private sector tenants' and are entitled to have their claims assessed within 14 days. In practice, local authority housing benefit departments rarely meet this deadline.

Payment of Housing Benefit

Local authorities often give higher priority to payments of benefit to their own tenants (for obvious financial reasons) and to private sector tenants (to minimise evictions) than they do to housing association tenants.

Once their claims have been assessed, housing association tenants are entitled to receive payment within a further 14 days. Again, in practice, this deadline is rarely met.

Problems also arise where payments which should have been made direct to the association are sent to the tenant instead. If the tenant spends this money, and the association cannot conclusively prove error by the local authority, the money may only be recoverable through the civil courts.

Housing Benefit Direct

Most housing associations welcome the payment of housing benefit direct to themselves as it helps to minimise rent arrears problems. However, the association only has the right to insist on this procedure if the tenant is in rent arrears of 8 weeks or more. Otherwise, the consent of the tenant is required before benefit can be paid directly to the association.

Benefit Reviews

Under the terms of the Housing Benefit (General) Regulations 1987, it is compulsory for claimants to have their benefit entitlement reviewed after a maximum of 60 weeks. Benefit payments are suspended while the review process takes place. In practice, local authorities normally review entitlement after 52 weeks for people whose income is unlikely to change and 26 weeks for people who are working or receiving occupational pensions. This procedure introduces the opportunity for further delays and uncertainty regarding benefit payment.

Why Do Problems Occur?

The key causes of difficulty are as follows.

Complexity Of The Benefit System

The method of claiming and calculating housing benefit entitlement is extremely complex and is difficult for tenants and assessment officers to understand.

Housing benefit was reviewed in April 1988 as part of a general Social Security Review exercise. One of the aims of the review was to simplify the system. However, initial success in this regard has been diluted by the frequency and extent of changes - not only in legislation but in revised guidance through Department of Social Security (DSS) circulars and amendments to its 'guidance manual'.

For example, benefit tapers have been changed regularly, hostel-dwelling claimants who received board and lodging allowances from the Department of Social Security were transferred to housing benefit in 1989, new rules regarding assessment of claimants' capital came into force in 1989 and student entitlement was all but eliminated in 1990. Many other changes have been made since 1988.

Particular problems have arisen because of the need for Income Support claimants to claim housing benefit and community charge (poll tax) benefit separately. Many claimants still do not realise this and consistently fail to return forms. This results in the cancellation of or delayed receipt of housing and community charge benefit payments.

Faulty Implementation of Benefit Procedures

In view of these changes it is not surprising that many local authorities have failed to keep up with developments and frequently misinterpret legislation - sometimes to the cost of claimants.

The relationship between over and under payments is a case in point.

Housing benefit staff can increase housing benefit entitlement retrospectively, but this power is limited to the previous 52 weeks. Conversely, there is no time limit on reclaiming overpayments.

However, the 52 week limit applies only where the local authority is required to pay money over to the claimant. By an arcane twist, the time limit does not prevent local authorities from looking further back when offsetting underpayments against overpayments, provided that the end result requires the claimant to pay at least some money back to the authority. However, many local authorities appear to be unaware of this distinction.

Clearly, local authorities should automatically offset any underpayments when calculating an overpayment.

Incentives to Reclaim Overpayments

Government subsidy rules regarding overpayments reward local authorities with 25% additional subsidy if they use their powers to reclaim money when overpayment is the claimant's fault. Some authorities have responded to this incentive by automatically invoicing housing associations for repayment of overpaid 'benefit direct'. If the association pays up, this may produce substantial arrears on the tenant's rent account. It may be impossible for the association to recover these arrears. However, the housing benefit regulations clearly state that associations are not legally obliged to repay benefit unless they could reasonably be expected to have known that a tenant's claim was inaccurate.

Reduction in Government Subsidy to Local Authorities

The ability of local authorities to provide an effective service has been undermined by changes in government subsidy entitlement. For example, from 1991-2 the subsidy available to authorities for housing benefit payments to private sector tenants will fall from 97% to 95% of benefit payments. The shortfall will have to be made up by reduced staffing or from local taxation - currently under review by central government!

Government subsidy towards costs resulting from backdated claims fell from 90% to 25% in April 1988, and this has naturally made local authorities more reluctant to backdate claims. The introduction of the 'good cause' principle at the same time has made it harder for claimants to argue for backdated payments and easier for authorities to refuse them. However, if 'good cause' is found, benefit should be backdated. Sadly, there is evidence that some authorities have adopted a blanket policies of not backdating payments.

Moreover, some authorities set a blanket ceiling above which they consider rents to be unreasonable, and thus restrict the level of rent upon which a claimants housing benefit entitlement is calculated. As a result, the claimant has to pay a higher proportion of rent in terms of net income and arrears are more likely to accrue. Some authorities apply these 'ceilings' to higher rented housing association property.

Such blanket policies are unlawful and should be avoided. They can also be challenged by claimants through the Review Board procedure.

Improved Liaison

By following the steps now suggested, housing association rent arrears can be substantially reduced.

Exchange of 'Organisational Charts'

Liaison between authorities and associations can be improved by the exchange of organisational charts which name the officers who are responsible (on the local authority side) for particular aspects of housing benefit administration and (on the housing association side) for arrears recovery and legal action. Associations would be justified in demanding that a senior housing benefit officer be assigned solely to liaison work.

Payments on Account

Where local authorities cannot process claims within 14 days, they should make greater use of their ability to provide 'payments on account' to private sector claimants. As has been noted, the term 'private sector claimant' includes tenants of housing associations. Some authorities have objected that this would mean that claims have to be assessed twice and would thus 'clog up the system'. However, if 'payments on account' were made on a flat rate basis this problem would not arise. Flat rate payments could be, for example, 100% of the claim if the claimant is in receipt of income support and the rent claimed is reasonable. Others could be paid 50% of the benefit claimed. Regulation 91 of the Housing Benefit (General) Regulations 1987 states that local authorities shall make payments on account to private sector tenants of sums which they consider reasonable, provided that the delay in assessing the claim is not the claimant's fault. Even where the claimant is at fault, but has good reason, (for example the self employed person who has not yet had their accounts audited and thus cannot supply relevant information), the authority is legally obliged to make a payment on account.

Improved procedures for reviewing Benefit Entitlement

In the case of periodic reviews of benefit entitlement, local authorities should adopt the following procedure.

Where the benefit review period is every 26 to 60 weeks, review forms should be sent to claimants 13 weeks before the review is due. The authority should monitor cases where no reply is received. Reminder letters should be sent four weeks later, pointing out that benefit will be lost unless a new claim is submitted. After a further four weeks, authorities should provide associations with a computer printout listing those of their tenants who have still not replied.

By analysing existing data regarding entitlement to pensions or benefit premiums which are related to disability, the computer should be able to identify vulnerable claimants. Staff from the association or the local authority housing benefit section should visit these tenants, particularly those who might not be able to understand the process or complete the form unassisted. Where housing association staff visit the claimant, the local authority can either accept their testimony of income and benefit entitlement or it can ask association staff to make a photocopy of relevant documents and send them to the housing benefit office for assessment. Housing association tenants who are not considered vulnerable may not merit a home visit, but a further reminder letter should be issued at this stage.

Where the benefit review period is less than 26 weeks, review forms should be issued at least 8 weeks before the review with follow up work following the pattern suggested above. Generally, however, local authorities should be encouraged to use the longer review periods for all claimants.

Adopting a consistent approach to Over and Under Payments

When reviewing benefits, local authorities should adopt a consistent approach to both underpayments and overpayments.

As mentioned earlier, the 52 week time limit period regarding underpayments only applies where money is actually owed to the claimant.

However, even here, there is room for local authority flexibility. The housing benefit department can invite a 'late appeal' from the applicant. Where such an appeal is made, the housing benefit officer dealing with the case has discretion over how far to backdate the increased benefit entitlement.

This procedure might, for instance, be invoked where the authority itself has been responsible for a mistaken assessment of a claimant's housing benefit entitlement. Where a 'late attempt' is made and the local authority makes an additional payment of benefit, it is entitled to claim 95% government subsidy towards the payment.

Liberal interpretation of Government Guidelines

Where backdating of benefit is concerned, local authorities are not bound to accept Department of Social Security (DSS) guidance on the interpretation of the 'good cause' principle. By taking a more flexible approach than that advocated by DSS the authority could assist tenants in avoiding arrears which may result in homelessness - and which may result in the authority having to rehouse the claimant (at even greater expense).

Further, under Regulation 69(8) of the Housing Benefit (General) Regulations 1987, local authorities can exercise their discretion and pay increased housing benefit in exceptional cases. This discretion is cash limited to 0.1% of the authority's housing benefit budget. However, if the budget is exhausted, staff can refer cases to the Review Board which can order payments without regard to budgetary considerations.

There is clearly scope for local authorities to be more flexible in dealing with individual claims.

Avoidance Of 'Blanket' Policies

Where a local authority applies a blanket 'ceiling' in determining the 'reasonableness' of housing association rents for housing benefit purposes, associations can and should challenge this action. Where local authorities automatically refer housing association tenants' claims to the Rent Officer, in order to obtain a market rent figure when assessing 'reasonableness', this will slow up the payment process. Again, associations should challenge such action, by pointing out that authorities have legal discretion over whether to refer such claims to the Rent Officer or not.

Role of Local Authority/Housing Association Liaison and Training Groups

Local Authority/Housing Association Liaison And Training Groups should spend more time on dealing with housing benefit problems, setting up sub-groups to deal with the subject in detail.

Welfare rights advisers have found a direct relationship between the simplicity of the local authority's benefit claim form and the degree of take-up. Associations, who may operate in other authority areas and have experience of claim forms which are better designed, should lobby the local authority to amend its claim form where necessary.

Housing associations operating in a local authority area should join together to share information on this issue. This will make any pressure they may apply, at officer or member level, for better procedures or improved staffing levels, more authoritative and effective. Associations will benefit from making a senior member of staff responsible for monitoring developments in housing benefit entitlement. This will enhance their ability to spot any failure of the local authority to implement new regulations or to interpret existing regulations correctly.

Associations should ensure that housing officers are adequately trained on all benefit issues, both to advocate tenants' claims and to negotiate effectively with the authority over matters such as payment on account, overpayments and 'use of discretion'. This in itself will help maximise rental income and should be part of any staff training on rent arrears recovery.

'Take Up' Campaigns

Associations should mount their own benefit take-up campaigns and should not leave responsibility for campaigns entirely to the local authority. Housing associations should hold stocks of housing benefit claim forms and advice leaflets to hand to their new tenants. Housing officers should explain the housing benefit system to tenants when they sign up and, at the same time, calculate their likely entitlement in order to demonstrate the benefit of making a claim.

Other Considerations

Associations can take legal action against local authorities or refer individual cases to the local government Ombudsman. Neither course of action is particularly satisfactory. Legal action may make it even more difficult to establish good working relationships with the local authority. The Ombudsman can take more than a year to make a decision!

Some local authorities are refusing to pay housing benefit unless claimants register for the community charge and some associations are issuing Notices Of Intention To Seek Possession at the same time as they sign tenants up. All such actions are unlawful and should be discontinued.

Example

Improved Liaison over Housing Benefit
London Borough of Lambeth

Housing associations operating in the London Borough of Lambeth had become increasingly concerned about housing benefit payments to their tenants. Delays of more than six months in benefit assessment and payment were common. LB Lambeth had been forced to disband its specialist 'housing associations housing benefit' unit, due to economies enforced by 'ratecapping'. Inevitably, this led to a further deterioration in the service.

Associations represented on the Lambeth Housing Associations Group (LAMHAG) considered various approaches to the problem and wrote collectively to the Chair of Housing expressing their concerns. As a result, significant improvements were made to the service.

The London Borough of Lambeth split its Housing Benefit Department into two divisions - public and private sector - with separate departmental heads. In the private sector division, individual officers were assigned to individual housing associations to facilitate better liaison. A specialist team was set up within the private sector division to sort out assessment problems concerning housing association tenants. LB Lambeth has also offered special advice and take-up sessions to housing association tenants where new schemes are being let.

The borough/association liaison group has established a sub committee, which is attended by appropriate senior officers and meets on a quarterly basis, to monitor liaison over housing benefit payment.

On its own, improved liaison would not have been enough. LB Lambeth also needed to introduce specific measures to make its housing benefit section more efficient. It did so by setting each member of staff a target workload and closely monitoring their performance. It also launched a massive 'take up' campaign targeted at public and private sector tenants. As a result, there has been an increase in both staff efficiency and the number of claims made. The backlog of claims has largely been cleared. Lambeth's

Housing Committee has instructed housing benefit officers to deal with claims within 14 days. Performance against this target is also being monitored closely.

LAMHAG has recently written to the Chair of Housing to acknowledge the improved service and to request that this improvement be maintained.

11

CONCLUSION

The Institute of Housing believes that, whoever the main provider of subsidised rented housing may be, responsibility for devising and co-ordinating a local housing strategy best lies with the local authority.

There are several reasons for this.

Local authorities will need to co-ordinate local housing strategy if they are to discharge their continuing responsibility under Part 3 of the Housing Act 1985 to obtain accommodation for homeless people, at a time when their resources are diminishing. Local authorities also have a continuing duty under Section 8 of the same Act to consider housing needs and conditions in their district, with respect to the provision of further housing accommodation.

Housing associations have no experience of this strategic role and, indeed, most associations would not seek it. Nor would it be appropriate. Associations vary in size, often specialise in various forms of housing provision, frequently operate across local authority boundaries on a national or regional basis and are not subject to the democratic accountability associated with local authorities. However, associations have specialist knowledge of particular types of housing need and provision which should be fed into the strategic plan.

Associations thus have a key role to play in assisting authorities to formulate a local housing strategy and in the practical business of implementing it. Indeed, in its 'Performance Expectations' document, the Housing Corporation states that associations have a duty to consider local housing needs, to co-operate with local authorities and to assist them in meeting their statutory responsibilities towards homeless people.

As has been demonstrated in this publication, there are many areas where authorities and associations can work together to implement a local housing strategy. In fact local authorities are, in the context of current government policy, reliant upon housing association capital resources and activity to implement any strategy in full. Equally, associations are often reliant upon local authority provision of land and financial assistance, the constructive use of planning powers and so on, if they are to produce housing at rents which people on low incomes can afford.

The Social Housing Contract

The Institute of Housing believes that this relationship is best expressed in the form of a 'social housing contract' between authorities and associations. This formal 'contract' will be far more positive and equal than the 'pacts' that have been signed in some areas following the Housing Act 1988 - many of which have had the effect of undermining the ability of local authority tenants to exercise Tenants' Choice. Like all good contracts it would contain a series of benefits and obligations for both parties.

The contract would be particularly effective if the appropriate Housing Corporation regional office was a co-signatory, although it is not suggested that the Corporation should be able to exercise a controlling influence over the terms of the contract. The social housing contract would encompass the following points:

■ The criteria to be applied by the local authority when deciding which housing associations a local authority is prepared to work with. The criteria might, for instance, require associations to have a track record of working in partnership with the authority (in terms of nominations and so on), to have a local office in or adjacent to the authority's area, to set up a local committee to manage housing stock in the area (where a national or regional association is concerned), to ensure that meetings of that committee are accessible to those tenants and other members of the local community who wish to attend, to have a demonstrable commitment to equal opportunities and to tenant participation in decision making, and to have a specific proportion of people who live in the local authority area on its central committee of management.

■ In return, the local authority would make specific commitments to associations which meet these criteria. These commitments would cover the sale of local authority owned land or housing, financial assistance, provision of renovation grants, the effective payment of housing benefit and so on. These commitments would cover the following three years, subject to review, to allow associations the luxury of some degree of forward planning. It would be most helpful if the regional office of the Housing Corporation was able to provide a corollary commitment to the allocation of HAG funding, as has occurred in the cases of the Leeds and Leicester consortia quoted in the chapter om 'Sale Of Local Authority Land'.

■ The associations would respond by making specific commitments (subject to review) in terms of nomination agreements, mutually agreed 'target rent' guidelines for new developments and relets, implementation of equal opportunity policies, implementation of tenant participation policies and so on.

■ The local authority, and associations party to the agreement, would approve arrangements for the monitoring of the contract to ensure that both sides have met their agreed commitments. Monitoring would take place on the basis of common, and mutually agreed, standards of performance. A crucial part of this monitoring would be research into the satisfaction of tenants and other members of the local community with the performance of both the authority and associations. This research should be supplemented by formal dialogue with local tenant organisations and community groups. In particular, the views of black and ethnic minority residents should be elicited.

■ Associations would be accorded a formal role in the development of the local authority housing strategy and housing capital programme, in terms of giving advice on needs and priorities.

6. In the spirit of partnership, this contract would be genuinely negotiated between the authority and associations. All terms would be open to annual renegotiation.

There may be some authorities and associations who might view such a contract as unnecessary and restrictive and who might argue that the present haphazard arrangements work well enough.

In anticipation of such objections, the Institute of Housing argues that difficulties would be outweighed by the following advantages.

Advantages For The Local Authority

■ the local authority can ensure that it is able to discharge its responsibilities towards homeless people

■ the local authority can influence rent levels on property to which homeless (and other) people are nominated

■ the local authority will be able to plan enabling activity in a more co-ordinated manner and to increase partnership activity with housing associations

Advantages For Housing Associations

■ associations will gain greater certainty with regard to future development opportunities

■ associations will gain greater influence over the payment of housing benefit to their tenants

■ associations with a track record of working in the area will be better protected against competition from larger or more asset-rich national or regional associations

■ unnecessary and destructive competition between local associations will be avoided

Advantages For Tenants And Other Members Of The Local Community

■ the views of tenants and other members of the community be part of an ongoing review of housing management performance and will thus help to raise standards in this respect

■ the performance of local housing associations with regard to equal opportunities and tenant participation will be monitored and there will be 'carrot and stick' inducements for associations to improve performance in this area and thus become more accountable to the local community

■ the performance of the local authority with regard to equal opportunities and tenant participation will be monitored and there will be 'peer group' pressure from housing associations for the local authority to improve its performance in these areas

Advantages For The Housing Corporation

■ the contract will maximise the opportunities for securing value for money in the application of Housing Association Grant (through the 'HAG stretch' mechanism identified in Chapter 1)

■ these contracts will assist the Housing Corporation in devising and implementing its regional investment strategies

Clearly, the precise terms of the 'social housing contract' would need to be freely negotiated at a local level, should not be unduly prescriptive and should be subject to annual review.

The Institute believes that this type of formal arrangement will ensure that local authorities and housing associations work together in an effective, fair and equal manner. After all, their housing objectives are almost synonymous.

Glossary

Assured Tenancy
A form of tenancy introduced for housing association and private sector tenants in the Housing Act 1988 which gives tenants fewer statutory rights than secure tenancies. Applies to all housing association lettings made after 15.1.89 except where secure tenants transfers within a housing association's stock.

Assured Shorthold Tenancy
A form of letting available to housing associations and private landlords, giving tenants fewer statutory rights than both secure and assured tenancies. The key factor is the ability of the landlord to regain possession automatically at the end of the tenancy term.

Basic Credit Approval
These are issued to local authorities every financial year by the DoE. They authorise the use of credit (primarily borrowing) to finance capital expenditure.

Capital Costs
Non-recurring expenditure on items such as housebuilding, purchase of vehicles and so on.

Capital Receipt
Payment which arises from the sale of capital items such as land or housing.

Compulsory Purchase Powers
Powers granted to local authorities to acquire unfit property for the purpose of rehabilitating or demolishing it.

Consideration
Legal jargon sometimes used, in the context of social housing, to describe payment for the sale of capital items or services. Consideration can be in the form of money, land, replacement housing or 'work in kind'.

Consortia
Formal partnerships between organisations to accomplish a specific task.

Cross Subsidy
Use of private sector subsidy to meet part of the costs of social housing schemes.

Decant
The process of moving a tenant out in order to demolish, repair or improve a property.

Direct Access Hostels
Hostels which offer emergency accommodation with no medium or long term right of occupation.

Fixed Equity
Limitation upon the right of the purchaser of a shared ownership dwelling to buy all of the equity (value) of the dwelling.

Floating Support
Support provided to people with special needs who live independently as opposed to living in hostels or institutions.

Fully Mutual Housing Society
A housing society whose rules restrict membership to persons who are tenants or prospective tenants of the society and which becomes eligible for tax concessions by doing so.

General Fund
The local authority account which receives community charge, uniform

business rate and central government subsidy payments. The money is used, in the main, to pay for the provision of local authority services.

Gratuitous Benefit

The sale of a local authority asset at less than its market value or the making of a local authority grant or loan to a private sector organisation.

Hostel Deficit Grant (HDG)

The system of Housing Corporation subsidy towards the revenue costs of special needs housing schemes which is being replaced with Special Needs Management Allowances.

Housing Association Grant (HAG)

Housing Corporation funding towards the capital costs of housing association schemes.

Housing Benefit Review Board

The panel of local authority councillors which acts as an appeal forum regarding the administration of housing benefit by the authority.

Housing Corporation

The government quango which provides capital and revenue funding for housing associations and housing co-operatives.

Housing Revenue Account

The local authority account which receives payments of rent and central government subsidy. The money is used to meet the revenue costs of managing and maintaining the authority's housing stock and paying housing benefit to the authority's tenants.

Joint Finance

The system of allocating a small and specific proportion of Department of Health funding. Decisions are made jointly by the local authority and the local health authority.

Liaison

Common term covering both the formal and informal relationship between organisations, such as local authorities and housing associations.

Local Authority HAG

Payments of HAG to housing associations by local authorities.

Mini-HAG

Capital funding provided by the Housing Corporation for short-life housing schemes.

Private Sector Leasing

The use of empty private sector property to provide temporary accommodation for homeless people.

Renovation Grants

Urban renewal grants paid by local authorities to private landlords and their tenants, housing associations and their tenants and owner occupiers for the purpose of rehabilitating or improving unfit dwellings.

Rent Officer

Inland Revenue employee responsible, amongst other tasks, for setting 'fair rents' rents for housing association properties let on secure tenancies.

Repair Notice

Notice issued by a local authority requiring the owner of an unfit dwelling to remedy its defects.

Revenue Costs

Recurring costs related to any form of business, charitable or public service activity. In terms of the provision of social housing, revenue costs would include staff salaries, day-to-day repairs and so on.

Shared Ownership

A method of acquiring part ownership of

a dwelling which is often employed by people who cannot afford outright purchase. Unsold equity normally remains with the organisation which constructed the dwelling – such as a housing association.

Short Life Housing
The use of empty local authority, housing association or private sector property to provide temporary accommodation.

Special Needs Management Allowance
The new system of Housing Corporation revenue funding for housing association special needs schemes introduced in 1991.

Staircasing
The process whereby a shared owner purchases further tranches of the equity of their home until they finally own the dwelling outright.

Subsidy
Financial assistance towards capital or revenue costs.

Tenants' Guarantee
The Housing Corporation charter of rights for assured tenants of registered housing associations.

Tenant Incentive Scheme
The system where Housing Corporation provides funding to housing associations in order to allow them to give a cash sum to tenants who wish to purchase private sector property.

thats the rule, but not always.